MASTERING CULTURAL DIFFERENCES

STRATEGIES FOR LEADING A GLOBAL WORKFORCE

LUIZA DREASHER, PHD

INDIE BOOKS INTERNATIONAL®

Printed in the United States of America.

ISBN-13: 978-1-952233-45-6
Library of Congress Control Number: 2021901876

To my husband David, I am thankful for the gift of your love and support. When life became challenging, you lifted me up, held me tight, and assured me it would all be okay. As usual, you were right.

To Monica and Camilla, you are the best daughters any parent could ask for. Keep pursuing your passion, making a difference, and reaching for your dreams. Know that you are truly amazing!

CONTENTS

PART I

Why Differences In The Workplace Matter And Why You Need To Master Them

CHAPTER 1

The Increasingly Diverse Work Environment

Companies must recognize that diversity is an imperative, not just something nice to do. The more diverse they are, the more successful they will be.

—Pat Russo, executive VP, Lucent Technologies

Imagine conducting an interview fully expecting the candidate to showcase their experience and skills. Much to your surprise, though, the expected bragging never takes place—almost as if the candidate were expecting you to recognize that their track record and seniority level should speak for themselves. During a performance review, you provide constructive criticism to an employee with the intent of helping him improve his performance. Later on, you learn that he quit his job because of the shame and loss of face your feedback caused. Your plan is to lead your staff meetings as usual—you expect all team members to make suggestions, participate freely, and demonstrate they can take the initiative. Yet, some of them never ask questions, rarely participate, make no contribution to the project, and never voice any complaints. This baffles you because you know how talented they are. Welcome to the new multicultural workplace!

The Impact Of Demographic Changes And Globalization

Historically, European-American men controlled and set the rules for corporate America. However, the workplace has been changing drastically in the last couple of decades, and demographic changes are one of the forces behind this shift.

According to projections by the US Census Bureau (Vespa, Armstrong, and Medina 2020, 6–7), the racial composition of the US population will change considerably in the coming decades.

> *One in three Americans—32 percent of the population—is projected to be a race other than White by 2060. The fastest-growing racial or ethnic group in the United States is people who are Two or More Races, who are projected to grow some 200 percent by 2060. The next fastest is the Asian population, which is projected to double, followed by Hispanics, whose population will nearly double*

> *within the next four decades. In contrast, the only group projected to shrink is the non-Hispanic White population. Between 2016 and 2060, the non-Hispanic White population is expected to contract by about 19 million people, from 198 million to 179 million, even as the total US population grows.*

The report also states that, by 2028, the foreign-born share of the US population is projected to be higher than any time since 1850. In fact, the number of immigrants living in the United States is projected to rise from 44 million in 2016 to 69 million by 2060. There is no denying that soon the United States will become a majority-minority nation.

Demographic changes inevitably impact the workplace. Compared to decades ago, today, we see a larger number of women and minorities in positions that were once out of reach. We are also seeing more individuals with disabilities, the LGBTQ+ community doesn't feel they have to hide their identities, and employees are living past traditional retirement age and choosing to keep working. In fact, according to a 2016 report published by Instructure, for the first time in history, we find four distinct generations (Baby Boomers, Gen X, Millennials, and Gen Z) at work—all partaking of the same break room, conference room, and training room.

As expected, they each bring along different expectations and priorities, and companies are being forced to adapt existing policies, programs, and procedures in order to better meet the diverse needs of these employees.

With the trend toward a more diverse workforce continuing, so are the ways we conduct business. In the past, most American businesses functioned primarily within US borders. Now, globalization is proving to be a huge game-changer for companies big and small. Globalization refers to the growing interdependence among people and cultures throughout the world (Bhucher 2008, 79). The technical capabilities we have available today—such as web conferencing, email, instant messaging, and many others—make it possible for individuals to communicate and collaborate across geographical boundaries. A staff meeting today can include team members in São Paulo, Quebec, and Mumbai. Many brands have also recognized the potential of a global market. Take Apple, for example, conceivably the world's most recognizable consumer tech brand, which now has retail stores around the world. According to Barbara Farfan (2019), as of 2018, Apple was operating 506 retail stores in twenty-five different countries around the world, in addition to the United States. The estimation is that more than one million customers visit Apple stores worldwide each day. This is more than double the attendance at all the Disney theme parks around the world combined. In Shanghai alone, more than 25,000 customers visit the Apple store every day, making it the busiest Apple store in the world.

A New Way To Work Together: From EEO To Inclusive Management

The traditional European-American leadership and management styles no longer apply to today's increasingly diverse workplaces. In the past, the expectation was that new hires would *melt* into the existing corporate culture. The problem was that people of color and women never "melted in" because they don't look or act like the dominant majority, Euro-American men (Carr-Ruffino 2015, 3). Fewer workers today are willing to give up significant parts of their identities for the sake of fitting into a corporate culture built primarily on values they cannot relate to—those of European-American men.

In *The Diversity Advantage: A Guide To Making Diversity Work*, Billings-Harris (1998) describes how diversity management changed through the years from government-mandated regulations to the need for the creation of a work environment that supports and challenges all individuals. The three stages are briefly discussed below.

Equal Employment Opportunity (EEO)

These were government-mandated regulations introduced as part of the Civil Rights Act of 1964. The goal was to create equal opportunities in hiring, development, and promotion for those who, in the past, were discriminated against because of the cultural group to which they belonged, such as people of color, women, people with disabilities, veterans, individuals of a certain religion, age, national origin, and others. Under these regulations, employers were required to provide an *equal opportunity* for these protected-class individuals who apply for positions or promotions. In theory, they are all equal.

Affirmative Action (AA)

The problem with EEO was that changes were too slow to materialize. Signed by President Lyndon Johnson in 1965, AA regulations required organizations to develop goals and strategies for hiring and promoting individuals who were within protected classes. The idea was that the workforce should mirror the community it serves. Unfortunately, AA became synonymous with quotas, and once companies reached numerical benchmarks, they felt they were done. It was also clear that just because the organization was more diverse, it did not mean they were inclusive since little or no attention was given to how people were treated once they were hired. The expectation was that once they joined the organization, they would assimilate into the organization's norms and values. In other words, the old melting pot mentality still prevailed.

Inclusive Management

While the recruitment of women and minorities increased, the same could not be said about their retention. Organizations then started implementing initiatives aiming at creating an inclusive environment. They recognized that valuing differences enabled them to create a more productive and profitable workplace. It is not, after all, about bringing in protected classes. It is about making sure differences are recognized and respected, which, in turn, translates into fewer lawsuits, lower turnover, and higher productivity. An inclusive organization is productive because individuals respect each other's differences and value all contributions. It is a place that celebrates differences instead of hiding or trying to change them. In essence, a place where individuals are not expected to give up who they are or leave significant parts of their identity behind in order to be productive.

Benefits Of A Multicultural Approach To Management

Leaders today recognize they cannot lead successful organizations unless they pay attention to demographic changes and globalization. Their organization's success depends on their ability to understand their diverse employees, customers, and global business partners. In fact, numerous research studies have confirmed the benefits of a multicultural approach to management. Some of these benefits will be discussed below.

1. Increased Recruitment And Retention Of Diverse Talent

This is possible as long as you and those around you are able to recognize differences and have the skills to work successfully across those differences. Meeting the needs of your diverse employees is essential because ethnic minorities are more resistant to fitting into a corporate culture that requires them to squelch important parts of their persona (Carr-Ruffino 2015, 15). The reality is that if you cannot meet the needs of your diverse employees, they are less likely to stay.

2. Increased Attraction Of Diverse Customers And Suppliers

Crockett (1999) argues that diversity is about ensuring that the workforce, as a whole, resembles the community it serves. Diverse employees are better able to relate to customers who are like themselves. Studies also show that diverse teams are more likely to produce products and services better tailored to diverse customers (Cox and Smolinski 1994). In fact, according to Carr-Ruffino (2015), a diverse workforce can provide cultural insight as to whether a product or service will meet the needs of diverse clients as well as how to best present the product to them. Furthermore, a diverse staff showcases the organization in a better light because it makes it a more attractive place to conduct business for a wider range of customers. Organizations that fail to pay attention to diversity issues end up losing the business of a larger, more diverse clientele (Losey 1993).

3. Increased Market Reach

Today, the combined purchasing power of the four major minority groups is not only huge but growing. According to the report, *The Multicultural Economy* (Humphreys 2019), in 2016, US Hispanic buying power was larger than the gross domestic product of Mexico. The report also shows that African American buying power, estimated at $1.2 trillion in 2016, will grow to $1.5 trillion by 2021, making them the largest racial minority consumer. In fact, the combined minority buying power is now $3.9 trillion. Companies that manage diversity effectively are better able to reap the benefits of the extraordinary economic power of US minority groups.

4. **Increased Problem-Solving And Innovation**

   Diverse teams display enhanced problem-solving, decision-making, and innovation. According to Mayo (1999), higher-quality decisions are made when different solutions are evaluated and weighted. Salomon and Schork (2003) also concluded that great decisions result from the merger of very different ideas. In fact, Chrysler VP James P. Holden said, "Teams become truly effective when they represent the full spectrum of diversity" (Carr-Ruffino 2015, 20). Diverse teams and organizations typically generate more options, especially more creative options, as well as higher-quality ideas. In addition, when opposing viewpoints are introduced, groupthink is less likely to take over (Nemeth 1986; Nemeth and Wachtler 1983; Cox, Lobel, and McLeod 1991; Watson, Kumar, and Michaelsen 1993).

5. **Increased Productivity**

   Effectively managing diversity helps diverse teams and individuals to be more productive once team members learn how to work successfully across their differences (Ely and Thomas 2001; Carpenter 2002). Productivity increases when individuals enjoy coming to work, feel happy to be working where they are seen as worthy and competent, and can relax into being themselves (Carr-Ruffino 2015,

20). Eisenberger, Fasolo, and Davis-LaMastro (1990) confirm that teams that are diverse in terms of ethnicity, age, values, background, and training are more productive and innovative than homogenous groups. In fact, they argue that diversity within a work team, if properly managed, will boost productivity and quality of output.

6. **Fewer Litigations And Problems With Image Loss**

The price of not managing diversity well is very high. In 2000, Coca-Cola agreed to pay $192.5 million to settle discrimination allegations in pay, promotions, and performance evaluations against Black employees. This was, at the time, the largest discrimination settlement in US history, according to Maharaj (2000). In 2018, Prada came under fire for its racist display of blackface dolls in SoHo. After investigating the brand for over a year, the New York City Commission on Human Rights reached an agreement with Prada requiring employees and executives in Milan and New York to undergo racial equity training and promote diversity and inclusion. This was a landmark deal since never before had a city agency forced an international brand to examine its own culture (Miller 2020). In 2019, Halliburton Energy Services, Inc. agreed to pay $275,000 to settle a national origin and religious discrimination lawsuit brought by the US Equal Employment Opportunity Commission (EEOC 2019).

7. Bottom Line: A Multicultural Approach To Management Increases Profit

Needless to say, the numerous advantages of effectively managing diversity add up for the reason a business is in business: making good profits (Carr-Ruffino 2015, 21). Organizations need to pay attention to the changing ethnic and cultural consumer market if they want to survive. Clearly, successfully engaging diversity in the marketplace is no longer an option for businesses; it is key to their economic survival. Organizations today have little choice but to diversify in order to remain profitable and sustain a competitive advantage (Richard 2017).

TIPS FOR MANAGING A MULTICULTURAL ORGANIZATION

- It is not about government-mandated regulations or achieving numerical benchmarks. It is about valuing differences that enables the creation of more productive and profitable workplaces.
- Because of increased diversity and globalization, you need a workforce who can work well across differences, can form productive relationships with diverse clients, and has the ability to help your company expand into diverse markets. To increase diversity recruitment, you must project and sustain a multicultural company image and recognize that talent is talent, no matter what it looks like. It is essential that your workforce resembles the market it serves.
- You need to abandon your ethnocentric thinking. Understand that your way is not the only way and not necessarily the best way.
- An inclusive organization is productive because individuals respect each other's differences and value all contributions. In essence, a place where individuals are not expected to give up

who they are or leave significant parts of their identity behind in order to be productive.

- Companies that manage diversity effectively are better able to reap the benefits of the extraordinary economic power of US minority groups.

- Teams that are diverse in terms of ethnicity, age, values, background, and training are more productive and innovative than homogenous groups.

CHAPTER 2

The Importance Of Mastering Cultural Differences

The main reasons why most businesses fail or are not profitable stem from the lack of understanding of how customers and employees think, what they want, and how they communicate.

—ICQ Global

My journey into the intercultural world began many years ago when I left Brazil to pursue my PhD in the United States. I remember very vividly the elation I felt when I first arrived. Everything was new and exciting: new food, new architecture, a new language, new culture, new possibilities. These feelings were in line with what cross-cultural adaptation literature describes individuals go through when they first arrive at their new destination. I was clearly in the honeymoon stage (Marx 2001). It wasn't until months into my journey that I started experiencing what I labeled *cultural dissonances*, although I could not quite figure out what was causing them.

When I first started school, I had to take the bus to the university. For the first couple of days, I kept missing the bus, which, inevitably, made me late for meetings and classes. My cultural informants, those I relied upon to help me navigate the new world, would inform me this could be easily remedied: figure out the route you need (which I did) and show up at the bus stop at the designated time. Any time after that, I would have to wait for the next bus. I remember scanning the detailed time table, seeing arrival and departure times such as 9:03 a.m., 11:27 a.m., 3:53 p.m., 7:39 p.m. for each of the designated stops and not being able to wrap my mind around it. *How is such precision possible?*

Although I learned to navigate the bus system, it was a little later into the semester that the time dissonance hit me again. I walked into my professor's office to ask a question about an upcoming assignment only to be told to come back during her designated office hours. Apparently, I walked in during her research time. I was floored! How much disruption would it have been for her to put aside her research for a minute, dissipate my worries, and go back to doing what she was doing? I could not understand why both things could not happen at the same time; more importantly, why was she so rigid about the way she dealt with time? While I learned to be more respectful of people's time in this country (I did not want to live through the embarrassment I suffered in my professor's office again), it wasn't until much later, when I started researching and teaching about cultural differences, that I could fully comprehend the reason behind my professor's behavior and my reaction to it—we both had different views of how we used time. And those differences were dictated by our cultures.

For over twenty years, I have been facilitating workshops for corporations, government, and nonprofit organizations, as well as educational institutions. Most of my workshops focus on the challenges of multicultural organizations and classrooms. Above all, I help clients recognize cultural differences and how they impact workplace interactions. I also share strategies on how to create more inclusive organizations that truly value cultural diversity so they can compete more successfully in a global economy.

As a facilitator, there is nothing more exhilarating than witnessing a client's *aha* moment. This happened to me during a workshop sponsored by the Employer Partners Council with representatives from Target, Pioneer Hi-Bred, Pella Corporation, and many other organizations. The workshop focused on diversity in the workplace, and one of the topics I discussed in the half-day training was the challenges of multicultural workplaces, including the many differences in communication styles, such as the ones discussed in Chapter 3.

At the end of the workshop, representatives from Pella Corporation pulled me aside to thank me for the insights I had provided. They went on to explain that they often had virtual meetings with their distributors around the world. Meetings with the Latin American team were often a source of great frustration for the US team, who tended to think of their interactions with the Latin Americans as *pulling teeth.* That is because this group tended to go around and around the issue instead of getting straight to the point. They also seemed to frequently veer off-topic, which the US Americans deemed a waste of their time. It wasn't until that morning they realized that the problem resided with their own lack of understanding of cultural differences—they had not realized that cultural differences in communication style even existed. While US Americans tend to be more direct communicators, that is, they tell it like it is and get straight to the point, many other cultures prefer a more indirect approach to communication.

And herein lies the essence of what will be discussed in this book: the importance of mastering cultural differences. In other words, the importance of identifying the cultural dissonances I mentioned and knowing how to shift your behavior accordingly. Because when you understand cultural differences, you are able to recognize when those differences are at the root of a problem. Ignoring differences can not only be disastrous on many levels but can also perpetuate discomfort within a global workforce. It is only after you learn about other cultures and how they differ from your own that you will become more comfortable and more effective in working across those differences.

The Meaning Of Culture

Carr-Ruffino (2015) suggests that culture impacts the way individuals feel, think, speak, and act. In essence, culture not only influences our behavior; it colors our interpretation of the behaviors of others. Interpreting our employees' or global partners' behavior from our own cultural perspective *will* lead to misunderstandings.

In 1976, Edward T. Hall introduced the notion of culture as an iceberg. His argument was that every culture has some aspects that are more visible than others; in the iceberg context, these are the aspects that sit above the surface. The *above-the-waterline* culture includes aspects such as language, architecture, music, clothing, etc. It refers to anything that can be perceived through the five senses. Most of an iceberg, though (about 90 percent), sits beneath the surface. These are the less-obvious aspects of the culture, such as notions of time, negotiation patterns, the importance of saving face, etc. These deep-surface aspects of culture constitute the foundation of what we see at the top. Understanding the underlying causes of why individuals behave the way they do will contribute to more effective interactions with employees, clients, and global partners. Figure 2.1 below is a representation of Hall's iceberg analogy for understanding the concept of culture.

The Need To Understand Cultural Differences

With increased diversity in the workplace and globalization, the potential for misunderstandings during interactions is high. First, language differences may lead to miscommunication and misinterpretation. Accents are hard to understand, especially when they come across the internet or hard-to-decipher telephone messages. Silence may be misconstrued as acceptance, and *Yes* is taken as *I agree with you* when it could just mean *Yes, I hear you.* In many workplaces, a group speaking in their native language during a break can be taken the wrong way: *Are they hiding something from me? Are they making fun of me (when there is laughter)?*

FIGURE 2.1: Representation Of Culture As An Iceberg

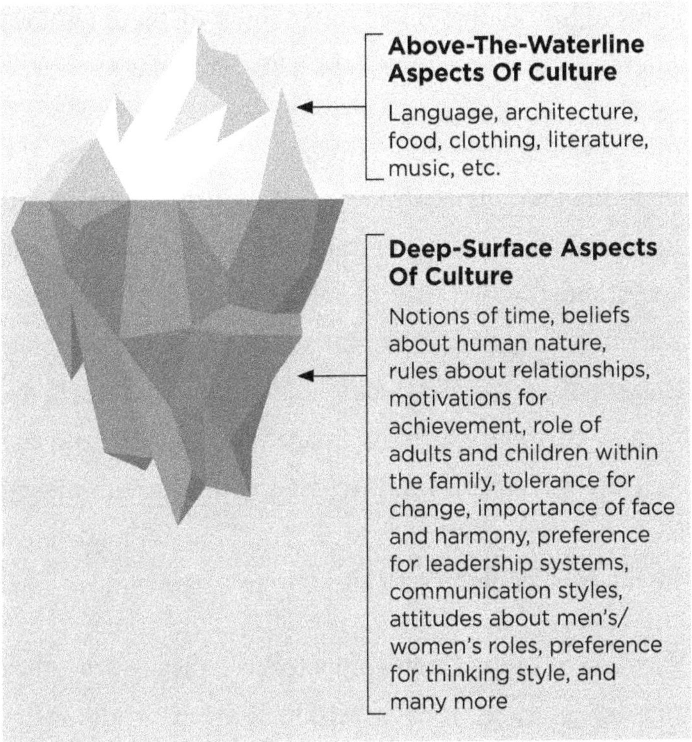
Above-The-Waterline Aspects Of Culture
Language, architecture, food, clothing, literature, music, etc.
Deep-Surface Aspects Of Culture
Notions of time, beliefs about human nature, rules about relationships, motivations for achievement, role of adults and children within the family, tolerance for change, importance of face and harmony, preference for leadership systems, communication styles, attitudes about men's/ women's roles, preference for thinking style, and many more

Adapted from Dreasher 2018

In Chapter 3, I cover the importance of understanding differences in communication styles.

Second, we fail to take into account the many differences in value orientation. People from other cultures often have values that differ from traditional US-American values. Mainstream Americans believe in individualism, egalitarianism, privacy, mobility, and materialism, some or all of which are not common to all cultures and lead to cultural clashes (Lambert and Myers 1994, 4). Chapters 4 through 7 in this book cover some of these cultural differences and how they impact the workplace.

Third, we ignore our unconscious bias toward the unfamiliar. We often fail to recognize that our thoughts and decisions are constantly influenced by our unconscious biases and that we tend to make decisions that impact individuals negatively without any awareness of our bias. The cost of unconscious bias in the workplace comes in the form of attrition, litigation, image loss, inability to relate with diverse customers, increased conflicts, diminished sales, and even career advancement. You will read about the full impact of unconscious bias in Chapter 8.

Needless to say, cultural competence skills are critical in this day and age. Today's workforce needs leaders who are aware that differences exist, know exactly what those differences are, and have the necessary skills to adjust their behavior to the cultural orientation of others (Dreasher 2010). When you understand cultural differences, you are able to recognize when those differences are the root of the problem. Imagine leaving a note to your Nigerian teammate, Ade, with a red pen—the only one you could find at the time. Later, your supervisor calls you into her office to find out what is going on between the two of you. Ade thinks you are mad at him. The problem resided not with the message but with the color of choice. For Nigerians, red carries a threatening overtone (Shutterstock 2015), and in some cultures, it symbolizes evil.

Likewise, the egalitarian approach of a US manager who rolls up his sleeves to work alongside his subordinates so the company can meet an upcoming deadline may be construed negatively by certain workers. Asian workers may see this behavior as an indication that their boss sees them as incompetent and that they will not be able to finish the project in time. The end result may be embarrassment, loss of face (discussed in Chapter 3), loss of respect for the manager, and, potentially, resignation. Cultural differences do matter!

Exporting your marketing campaigns to another country without taking cultural differences in the target country into account can also be disastrous, as documented in global business literature. Ricks (2006) reports that an American multinational company tried to sell baby food in Africa by using its regular label, which showed a smiling baby. Unfortunately, the local population interpreted things differently. For them, the jars contained ground-up babies. Needless to say, sales did not go as expected.

Animals are common in advertising in the US, and we can find ads including different types of animals ranging from dogs (i.e., Taco Bell's Chihuahua) to a gecko (Geico's mascot). In certain countries, though, using dogs in your marketing campaign would be disastrous. Morrison and Conaway (2011), in their book *Kiss, Bow, or Shake Hands: Sales and Marketing,* shared the story of a US real estate executive joyfully handing out business cards at a conference in the Arabian Gulf and being surprised by the negative response they evoked. His card, mind you, featured him with his beloved dog. The problem is that dogs are considered unclean in much of the Middle East.

Likewise, Nike was forced to recall thousands of pairs of shoes because the logo on the back was designed to resemble fire. However, when viewed from right to left, the way Arabic is read, it resembled the Arabic word for Allah (Morrison and Conaway 2006). Muslims saw this as a desecration of Allah's name (by placing it on a product). Equally disrespectful was the fact that it appeared on something that covers your feet. According to Hoeller (2015), in many Arab, Muslim, Hindu, and Buddhist countries, showing the soles of your feet is disrespectful since they are the dirtiest part of your body.

Only when managers and supervisors understand the impact of culture in the workplace, marketing campaigns, and negotiations will they be able to leverage those differences to create an advantage for their organizations. Ignoring differences can not only be disastrous on many levels but can perpetuate the discomfort within a global workforce. Thiederman (1991, 10) argues that by noticing and learning about other cultures, we become more comfortable with diversity, and therefore, more willing to seek out diverse clients and customers and more willing to hire culturally different workers.

Before moving forward, a word of caution: It is important to understand that the cultural differences discussed in this book are to be seen as generalizations and do not apply to all individuals in all contexts. Treat them as zip codes instead of exact addresses. That is because there are always individuals whose behavior varies from generalizations.

TIPS FOR WORKING WITH DIVERSE EMPLOYEES AND CLIENTS

- Recognizing cultural differences is okay. You are simply acknowledging that differences exist. You need to leverage the cultural diversity within your organization, not ignore it.
- Understand that there are many possible ways of achieving success; your way is just one possible way. It is essential to consider different perspectives. The best solution will be the one that is aligned with all different orientations involved.
- Understand that a culture-blind approach is no longer feasible in today's culturally diverse workplace.

PART II

CULTURAL DIFFERENCES THAT IMPACT THE WORKPLACE

CHAPTER 3

Differences In Communication Styles

The problem with communication is the illusion that is has been accomplished.

—George Bernard Shaw

Cultural Incident: Doing Business In China**

Gabriel, sales manager at Ready to Golf, was excited to be in Beijing attending China's largest trade show of sporting equipment. He was known for being a team player and a hard worker for his company. But Gabriel had the undeserved misfortune of being sent to China while speaking next to no Mandarin, aside from *ching* (please) and *xièxie* (thank you).

Ready to Golf specializes in golfing equipment, including unique and personalized golf head covers. Golf is a growing industry in China, with numerous golf courses in the process of being established. With close to 400,000 players over the age of eighteen, more than

400 golf courses, and about 100 others currently under construction, Gabriel was excited about the prospect of extending his company's business operation to China.

On the first day at the show, Gabriel mostly looked around at the various exhibits and gathered ideas of whom to approach. The next day, he was ready to test his selling skills. He approached Mr. Huang, general manager at China Golf, China's largest superstore, which carries all of golf's biggest name brands. Their recent acquisition by Top Golf USA was sure to expand their operations even more. Gabriel was certain his company's unique golf head covers would be of interest to the growing Chinese golf market.

From reading about the Chinese culture, Gabriel knew that getting down to business immediately after introducing himself would not be appropriate. His first order of business was to establish some sort of relationship with Mr. Huang. Because time was of the essence, after a little while, Gabriel expertly guided the conversation to the topic of how Mr. Huang's company could position itself in the cutting edge of the golf world by selling some of Ready to Golf's personalized golf head covers. He then suggested they meet so Gabriel could provide him with detailed information about his company and their unique products.

Mr. Huang responded, “That is interesting.”

Gabriel sensed this was a sign the conversation was going in the right direction and jumped at the opportunity. “When can we meet?”

“Life is very busy this time of the year.”

Gabriel agreed (he was also busy) but felt best to strike while the iron was hot. “How about tomorrow morning at 9:00 a.m.?”

Mr. Huang was pensive then said, “Tomorrow? Maybe I have time.”

“I will only need thirty minutes of your time. I can meet you here.”

Mr. Huang, still pondering, questioned, “Tomorrow at 9:00 a.m.?”

“Yes, 9:00 a.m. Will I see you then? You will not regret this!”

“Okay, sure, why don’t you come by tomorrow?” It wasn’t the enthusiastic response Gabriel was hoping for, but he would take it.

Gabriel was excited about the possibility of doing business with Mr. Huang. This could finally be the professional break he has been waiting for. If all went well, it was sure to put him on the fast track to a senior sales manager position in his company.

At 9:00 a.m. the next day, he approached Mr. Huang's exhibit only to be told that Mr. Huang had some other important business to attend to and would not be able to meet with him. Despite his disappointment, he was not giving up. He approached Mr. Huang's secretary in the hopes of rescheduling the appointment only to be told that Mr. Huang was not available at all in the next couple of days.

Gabriel was frustrated. Above all, he could not understand why Mr. Huang lied to him.

**Adapted from Wang, Brislin, Wang, Williams, and Chao*

What To Consider When Communicating Across Differences

Communication is the process by which we exchange ideas, feelings, and symbols of all kinds in a way that can be understood by others (Bucher 2008, 129). The way we communicate, including when, where, and how we should deliver the message, is deeply influenced by our culture.

Effective communication in a multicultural setting can be challenging. Workers may not comprehend instructions;

customer service personnel may find difficulty describing their products to prospective clients, and sales managers wonder if crucial details of contract negotiations are being misunderstood (Thiederman 1991). That is not all. A foreign-born customer may not ask important questions about a product or a needed service for fear of not being able to understand the answer. A colleague may hesitate to speak up in a meeting, worrying that his thick accent may not be understood. There is also the concern of others perceiving you as slow, inarticulate, or uneducated—perceptions which, according to Thiederman (1991), inevitably generate feelings of inadequacy and low self-esteem in those who do not speak the native language.

Differences In The Way We Communicate

To communicate successfully across differences, you need to (1) learn about different styles, and (2) avoid projecting your style onto someone else. The following style differences are worth mentioning because of their potential for creating misunderstandings in the workplace and in business negotiations.

Direct Versus Indirect Communication

Consider the following example:

> *Three Indonesian students living in the United States were invited by their advisor to participate*

> *in a cross-cultural training workshop. They did not want to participate, nor did they have the time. But they did not want to offend their professor, whom they held in high regard. Rather than tell the professor they couldn't attend, they just didn't return his calls and didn't show up to the workshop. (Martin and Nakayama 2000, 157–158)*

The direct/indirect continuum refers to the extent speakers reveal their intentions through verbal or written communication. Direct communicators, which many individuals in the United States consider as the most appropriate in the majority of contexts, disclose their needs and intentions in their message. Indirect communicators, on the other hand, tend to camouflage (Martin and Nakayama 2000) their needs and intentions. For cultural groups who prefer this style, preserving harmony in the relationship is more important than being totally honest. A white lie, like the one told by the students above, would be far more appropriate than telling the truth, which could offend or disappoint their professor.

Scholars (Gudykunst 2004; Ting-Toomey and Chung 2012; Dreasher 2018) have highlighted key differences between direct and indirect communicators.

Direct Communicators

- Say what they mean and mean what they say.
- See no need to read between the lines.
- Believe it is best to tell it like it is.
- Are less likely to imply and more likely to say what they are thinking.
- Are likely to mean *yes* when they say *yes*.

Indirect Communicators

- Don't always say what they mean or mean exactly what they say.
- Require that listeners read between the lines.
- Are more likely to suggest or imply than to come out and say what they think.
- Feel they can't always tell it like it is for fear it will upset the other person.
- May mean *maybe* or even *no* when saying *yes*.

Table 3.1 below shows where different countries fall on the direct/indirect continuum. Please note that these placements are approximations and that they indicate the position of a culture as a whole on these matters, not of individuals (Storti 1999, 99).

TABLE 3.1: Position of selected cultures in the direct/indirect continuum

Adapted from Storti 1999

The Role Of Context In The Communication Process

Consider the interaction between these two Japanese women:

Mrs. Tran: *Hello, Mrs. Nguyen…Your son Minh-Ha is entering his high school karaoke contest, isn't he? I envy you because you must be so proud of his talent. You must be looking forward to his future as a pop singer…I am really impressed by his enthusiasm—every day, he practices so hard, for hours and hours, until late at night…*

Mrs. Nguyen: *Oh, I'm so sorry…Minh-Ha is just a beginner in karaoke singing. We don't know his future yet… He is such a silly boy singing so late. We didn't realize you can hear all the noise next door. I will tell him to stop right away. I am so sorry for all your trouble; it won't happen again.* (Ting-Toomey and Chung 2012, 124)

A significant way in which groups differ in the way they communicate relates to their preference for high-context or low-context communication. For high-context communicators, most of the information is either in the physical context or internalized in the person, while little is in the coded, explicit, transmitted part of the message (Hall 1976, 79). The listener's primary task is to understand what is being said beyond the verbal message or through nonverbal channels. As illustrated in the exchange above, for certain groups, **body language, context, and environmental clues carry the message across.** Mrs. Tran used indirect hints and nonverbal signals to get her point across. However, Mrs. Nguyen immediately understood the message by reading between the lines of Mrs. Tran's comments: her son's late-night practices were disturbing Mrs. Tran. To preserve the relationship and avoid a potential conflict, Mrs. Nguyen apologized to her neighbor.

While high-context communicators are encouraged to pay close attention to body language and other environmental cues outside of the verbal messages such as social roles or positions, low-context communicators do the opposite. For them, the majority of the information should be transmitted through explicit verbal messages. Intercultural communication researchers (Martin and Nakayama 2000; Gudykunst and Matsumoto 1996) have found that, in the United States, the tendency is to avoid relying on nonverbal, contextual information; instead, individuals should be explicit, to the point, and not leave things ambiguous (Martin and Nakayama 2000, 156).

Scholars (Dreasher 2018; Ting-Toomey and Chung 2012; Samovar and Porter 1997) summarize both styles of communication as follows:

High-Context Communication Style

- Intentions are best conveyed through the context (e.g., social roles, status, or positions) and through nonverbal channels (e.g., pauses, silence, tone of voice).
- Preference for an indirect mode of communication as well as a roundabout way of expression.
- The receiver is responsible for reading between the lines and deciphering the hidden or contextual meanings of the message.

Low-Context Communication Style

- Intentions are best expressed through explicit verbal messages.
- Preference for direct verbal mode or straight talk.

- The speaker is responsible for constructing a clear, persuasive message that the listener can easily decode.

Table 3.2 lists the country examples of low- and high-context communication.

Table 3.2: Position of selected countries in the low- and high-context communication continuum.

Low-Context Communicators	←	→	High-Context Communicators
Germany	Unites States	Saudi Arabia	Japan
Switzerland	Canada	Kuwait	China
Denmark	Australia	Mexico	South Korea
Sweden	United Kingdom	Nigeria	Vietnam

Ting-Toomey and Chung 2012

In multicultural workplaces or when working with overseas partners, it will pay handsomely to understand the role of context in your conversations. Never go into a conversation or business negotiation, expecting that everything will be up-front or communicated to you directly. When working with high-context employees or partners, remember to read between the lines and decode the nonverbal subtleties that are, no doubt, accompanying their verbal messages. Likewise, high-context communicators need to learn to work more effectively with those on the opposite end of the continuum. They need to practice expressing their intentions through explicit and direct verbal messages and delivering direct, clear, persuasive messages.

Yes Doesn't Always Mean Yes

Martin and Nakayama (2000, 158) reported that

> *"[A}n international student from Tunisia had been in the United States for several months before he realized that if one was asked directions and didn't know the location of the place, one should tell the truth instead of devising a response. He explained he had been taught it was better to engage in conversation, to give a person some response than to disappoint the person by revealing that he didn't know."*

When preparing international TAs (teaching assistants) to teach in the US, I encountered the same problem. Many of my trainees felt that, when asked a question they did not know the answer to, the best course of action would be to provide an answer, even if they were not sure it was the right one. In their minds, any answer was better than no answer at all. In fact, not answering or saying they did not know would inevitably result in losing the respect of their students.

The reality is that, in some cultures, it is inappropriate to say *no*, so the tendency is to soften an upcoming negative answer or statement. An employee with an Asian cultural background might, for example, avoid saying *no* by answering a question with another question. A Middle Eastern colleague may say, “Maybe I can do it, I’ll let you know,” even though he knows it is impossible. Oftentimes, *yes* simply means, “Yes, I understand or hear you” and not necessarily, “Yes, I agree with you.”

These types of behavior are often misconstrued, despite the fact that the individual may be using such tactics as a means of avoiding confrontation, being seen as rude, or even causing disappointment, as in the situation of the Tunisian student above. When working across cultures, managers and supervisors need to be aware of the tendency of softening the negative by certain groups and understand that responses such as *maybe*, *perhaps*, *it's difficult*, or *I will consider it*, actually mean *no* for some of them. According to Dreasher (2018), a more effective strategy in situations like this is to avoid asking yes-or-no questions altogether. Instead, provide multiple options so employees can reject what they do not want without feeling they have caused offense or disrupted the harmony of the relationship.

The Importance Of Saving Face

Saving face is a concept that is often misunderstood in the West. In fact, researchers have found that US Americans place nowhere near the same emphasis on saving face as do Asians, Middle Easterners, and Hispanics. Table 3.3 below shows the position of selected cultures as it relates to the importance they place on saving face.

This concept is based on the fact that none of the parties in a relationship or situation should suffer embarrassment. This is why a Korean passed over for a promotion is likely to quit his job rather than endure embarrassment if he stays with the company. Likewise, a supervisor's suggestion for improvement, even if offered in a courteous manner, may be taken as an insult by a Hispanic employee. Thiederman (1991, 109) contends that ignoring this concept can have an immediate and destructive impact on those involved.

Storti (1999) argues that, for groups whose members value saving face:

- preserving harmony is a key concern
- *adjusting* the truth is preferable, especially if it threatens someone's face
- saying what you think the other person wants to hear is the best approach

- disagreeing, confronting, or saying no should be avoided because it disturbs the harmony of the relationship

On the other hand, for groups who place less importance on face:

- telling the truth is more important than sparing someone's feelings
- honesty is the best policy
- it's okay to say no or to disagree with individuals
- receiving and efficiently providing information is the primary goal of the communication exchange

TABLE 3.3: Position of selected cultures according to the importance they place on saving face.

Face Less Important				Face More Important
Germany United States	United Kingdom France Russia	Middle East India Mexico Spain	Africa China Southeast Asia	Japan

Thiederman (1991) argues that the desire to save face is manifested in a number of behaviors—each reflecting a different concern. For example, employees who are reluctant to admit a lack of understanding may do so for fear of appearing ignorant. Those who avoid taking the initiative may do so for fear of performing the task the wrong way and risking embarrassment. Likewise, some employees may avoid asking for a promotion for fear of humiliation if turned down.

The Use Of Silence

For US Americans, silence can feel uncomfortable or awkward because it possibly signifies a breakdown in the communication process. Therefore, they tend to fill those awkward moments with uncertainty-reduction strategies (Gudykunst 2004), such as asking questions. For many other groups, though, silence communicates respect and deference. These groups tend to reduce uncertainty by means of silence, observation, or even asking someone else about a behavior they observed.

When dealing with a culturally diverse workforce, managers and supervisors need to understand that silence communicates as much as the spoken word. It is an important aspect of the communication process for certain groups, and they need to become more comfortable with the absence of words. As Dreasher (2018) points out, the silent employee in the staff meeting may well be trying to understand what is being said (e.g., translating) or taking time to formulate a question or a response. While silence can sometimes indicate that something has gone wrong, it is also possible that it is being utilized to achieve better communication.

Cultural Incident Revisited

There are two important cultural aspects of the interaction between Gabriel and Mr. Huang. The first one has to do with the communication style used by both parties. As we have seen in this chapter, US Americans prefer a more direct approach while the Chinese are more comfortable with indirectness and ambiguity.

The second cultural aspect that Gabriel ignored was the one of saving face, which is often misunderstood by US Americans. As we discussed, it involves the notion that none of the parties in a relationship or situation should suffer embarrassment. Mr. Huang was probably not interested in the product Gabriel was introducing but chose an indirect way to relay his message.

The signs were clear. A Chinese person or someone versed in differences in communication styles would have picked up on the fact that Mr. Huang's answer, *Life is busy this time of the year*, was his indirect way of showing he was not interested in Gabriel's products. Rejecting Gabriel's products outright would cause Gabriel to lose face. The best solution, then, was simply not to show up for the meeting.

It is clear that Gabriel did not have the cultural savvy to interpret Mr. Huang's different communication style correctly.

TIPS FOR COMMUNICATING EFFECTIVELY ACROSS DIFFERENCES

- In the United States, remember that the preferred style of communication in most situations is the direct style.
- Recognize that different groups place different values on telling the truth, being honest, preserving harmony, and avoiding conflict.
- Keep in mind the tendency of some groups to soften a negative answer.
- Understand that responses such as *maybe*, *perhaps*, *it's difficult*, or *I will consider it*, actually mean *no* for some of them.
- Avoid asking yes-or-no questions. Instead, provide individuals with options so they can reject what they do not want without feeling

they have offended you or disrupted the harmony of the relationship.

- Remember that US Americans place nowhere near the same emphasis on saving face as do other groups. For some, sparing someone's feelings is more important than telling the truth. Honesty is not always the best policy. In fact, preserving harmony and saving face for all parties is the main goal.

- Recognize the need that some groups place in saying what the other person wants to hear.

- Know that cultural groups differ in the relative importance placed on speaking and silence. For some groups, silence is seen as a possible breakdown in the communication process. For others, silence is a sign of respect or admiration. It is also possible employees are using silence to achieve better communication.

- Remember that silence can communicate as much as the spoken word. The silence on the part of your Asian employee could be him showing respect, or it could be reluctance to stand apart from other colleagues.

CHAPTER 4

The Importance Of Nonverbal Communication

When the eyes say one thing and the tongue another, a practical man relies on the language of the first.

—Ralph Waldo Emerson

Cultural Incident: What Went Wrong?

For the last five years, Caroline has been working as a manager at BCL Technologies in Texas. BCL Tech, a large electronics firm, has dozens of locations throughout the world and provides product design and prototyping, manufacturing, and fulfillment to customers worldwide. BCL also serves diverse markets, including medical, communications, environmental, transportation, agricultural, and military.

The best part of Caroline's job is interacting with her diverse workforce. In fact, for the last couple of years, BCL has become increasingly diverse due to the growing number of immigrants moving to the area. There are some drawbacks to her job, though. Because of language differences, Caroline often finds herself choosing her words carefully when passing on instructions. She has also learned to stop frequently during staff meetings to check for understanding. Another strategy she has utilized with her crew is using a lot of gestures to go along with her vocal instructions.

Haziq, an electronics assembler at BCL who immigrated from Malaysia, was due for his quarterly performance evaluation with Caroline. When he arrived at her door, Caroline beckoned him to come in. Clearly, something went wrong because Haziq looked offended by the invitation.

What could have possibly gone wrong?

The Importance Of Nonverbal Communication

Nonverbal communication, simply put, is communication without words (DeVito 1989, 3). How we look, how we move, how we sound, the way we touch, whether or not we maintain eye contact during a conversation, the speed at which we speak, how loud or soft we speak, even how we use space and time are all part of the nonverbal messages we send and receive (Singelis 1994).

Researchers agree that nonverbal communication carries far more weight than verbal communication. Although estimates vary from 50 percent (Thiederman 1991) to 65 percent (Birdwhistell 1955) to 93 percent (Mehrabian and Ferris 1967; Singelis 1994), there is an agreement that the majority of what we communicate is done through nonverbal channels.

Nonverbal communication can become especially problematic in business negotiations or workplace situations where more than one culture is involved. That is because, regardless of what you intend to communicate, your behavior can be interpreted by others differently. Take, for example, touch behavior between a man and a woman. Touch can be particularly troublesome since the intentions of the person initiating the touch may be received quite differently by the person being touched.

Cultural Differences In Nonverbal Behavior

Differences In The Use Of Time

One important aspect of nonverbal communication refers to the use of time. Hall identified two major patterns in the use of time: monochronic and polychronic. Like oil and water, they don't mix (Hall 1983, 45–46).

There are many cultural variations regarding how these two groups understand and use time. Here is a summarization of the significant differences between them:

Monochronic Orientation

- Time is a commodity. We can save, gain, lose, spend, or waste it.
- Time is linear, with one event happening at a time (e.g., If I am meeting with a client, I should not interrupt the meeting to take a phone call).
- The needs of people are subservient to the demands of time.
- Deadlines, schedules, and keeping to the task are important.
- People may be too busy to see us.
- To be late or kept waiting is rude.
- Work time is distinguished from social time.

Polychronic Orientation

- Time is limitless and not quantifiable. There is always more time.

- Time is viewed as more holistic. Many events can happen at once (e.g., socializing during a meeting is not only accepted but expected).
- People are never too busy. Schedules, appointments, and deadlines are easily changed.
- Relationships are more important than keeping to the task. Plans are fluid. There is no such thing as an interruption.
- To be late or kept waiting is okay.
- Work time is integrated with social time.

Figure 4.1 shows a visual representation of where countries fall on the monochronic/polychronic continuum.

FIGURE 4.1: Where Countries Fall In The Monochromic/Polychromic Continuum

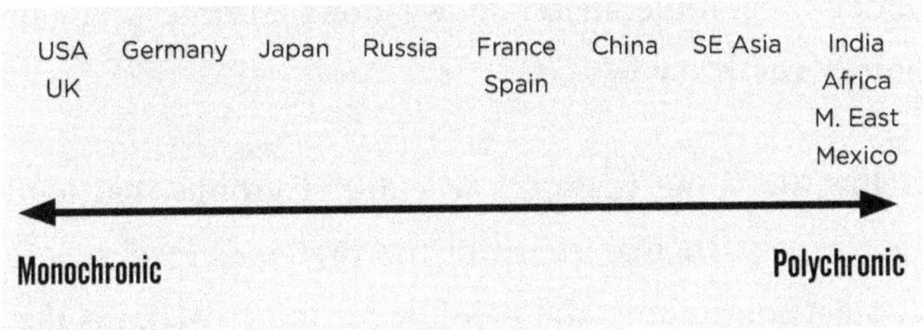

Adapted from Storti 1999

International visitors often complain that US Americans seem too busy, too tied to their schedules; they complain that US Americans do not care enough about relationships and about the personal aspects of living (Martin and Nakayama 2000, 187). It is important to keep in mind that, whatever our time orientation, issues are likely to surface in interactions with employees who have the opposite orientation—especially as it relates to keeping appointments.

Variations In Eye Contact

Cultures vary as far as patterns of eye contact. Because of that, we not only have to pay attention to how long the gaze is held (e.g., from direct to minimal eye contact) but also to the roles the parties are playing in the conversation (Thiederman 1991). For some groups, avoiding eye contact is a way of showing respect and admiration. For others, the exact opposite is true. In our increasingly multicultural workplaces, it is imperative that we learn about these differences, so we don't misinterpret our employees' behavior.

Below are some examples of cultural groups that tend toward a particular range in the preferred level of eye contact continuum, and possible misinterpretations that might occur (adapted from Thiederman 1991).

Prefer Very Direct Eye Contact

Groups	Middle Easterners, some Hispanic groups, the French
Actual Intention	Desire to express interest; desire to communicate effectively
Possible Misinterpretation	Hostility, aggressiveness, intrusiveness, bossiness

Prefer Moderate Eye Contact

Groups	Mainstream US Americans, Northern Europeans, the British
Actual Intention	Desire not to appear aggressive or intrusive
Possible Misinterpretation	Lack of interest in what is being said

Prefer Very Minimal Eye Contact

Groups	East Asians, Southeast Asians, East Indians, Native Americans
Actual Intention	Desire to show respect and not to be seen as intrusive
Possible Misinterpretation	Lack of interest, dishonesty, lack of understanding, fear, shyness

Handshakes And Other Forms Of Greeting

A proper handshake is a function of an individual's culture. In other words, a supervisor's idea of an appropriate handshake may not necessarily match that of the employee he or she is meeting. Researchers have found that in the US, a firm handshake accompanied by direct eye contact is expected in business interactions. For Middle Easterners, on the other hand, a gentle grip would be more appropriate since a firm grip suggests aggression (Thiederman 1991).

Shaking hands is an art, so to speak. You have to consider who you shake hands with, when, how often, as well the firmness of your grasp. Table 4.1 below shows variations in what is considered an appropriate handshake across different groups.

It is also important to realize that a handshake is not a universal form of greeting. In Japan, the customary form of greeting is to bow. In India, on the other hand, the *namaste* (hands placed in a praying position, chest high, accompanied by a slight head bow) is the appropriate greeting. In the Middle East, the *salaam* (with the right hand, touch the heart then the forehead and sweep the hand upward), often accompanied by *salaam alaykum* (peace be with you), is expected.

TABLE 4.1: Variations In Handshake Across Cultures

US Americans	Firm
Germans	Brisk, firm, repeated upon arrival and departure
French	Light, quick, not offered to superiors, repeated upon arrival and departure
British	Soft
Hispanics	Moderate grasp, repeated frequently
Middle Easterner	Gentle, repeated frequently
Asians	Gentle; for some, shaking hands is unfamiliar and uncomfortable (an exception: Koreans generally have a firm handshake)

Adapted from Thiederman 1991

To give you a sense of the extreme variations in greeting behavior, and as a reminder to never project your form of greeting onto someone else, consider the examples below. According to Axtell (1991):

- Eskimos greet each other by banging the other party with a hand either on the head or shoulders.
- Polynesian men welcome each other by embracing and then rubbing each other's back.

- Among the Matavai, friends scratch each other's head and temples with the tip of a shark's tooth.
- The Maori of New Zealand rub their noses when greeting.
- Among some African tribes, it is appropriate to spit at each other's feet.
- Tibetan tribesmen stick out their tongues at each other.

Other Hand Gestures

In addition to handshakes, there are many variations in hand gestures that can cause misunderstandings. Consider the following example:

> *An American teenager was hitchhiking in Nigeria. A carload of locals passed him. The car screeched to a halt. The locals jumped out and promptly roughed up the visitor. Why? Because in Nigeria, the gesture commonly used in America for hitchhiking (thumb extended upward) is considered a very rude signal. (Axtell 1991, 7)*

People all over the world use their hands to aid in the communication process. The problem is that many gestures mean different things to different groups, as in the example above. When communicating, it is important to become more conscious of these differences because our gestures can be misinterpreted. When using certain gestures, Thiederman (1991) suggests we keep the following cultural differences in mind.

Pointing. Often considered poor etiquette in the US. Likewise, to point at an Asian with the index finger is offensive and intrusive. In Thailand, China, and many other Asian countries, pointing is done with the entire hand. In Malaysia, however, pointing is done with the thumb.

Beckoning. Mainstream US Americans beckon to others with upturned fingers, palm facing the body. This same gesture is considered offensive to Mexicans, Filipinos (this is how they beckon to animals or sex workers), and Vietnamese.

Gestures Of Validation. The okay sign, the thumbs-up signal, and the V for victory (done with the palm facing the face) are offensive to many cultures. All three have sexual connotations, as does the thumbing a ride gesture (Thiederman 1991, 140).

Left Hand. While many US individuals may not think much of it, gesturing or handing something with the left hand is offensive to many Muslims as this is regarded as the toilet hand (Thiederman 1991, 140), for hygiene after the use of the toilet. The right hand is the one used for all social functions such as shaking hands, eating, or handing something to another person.

The Legs And Feet

Lastly, while the US does not have an etiquette rule regarding the proper positioning of the legs, the same cannot be said for other cultures. In fact, some cultures have fairly strict rules of leg and feet etiquette. For Middle Easterners and Asians, for example, crossing the legs is not appropriate; when the leg is crossed, the bottom of the foot is showing, which is considered rude and offensive. The same can be said for placing the ankle on the knee.

Cultural Incident Revisited

A common beckoning gesture in the United States is for individuals to curl their index finger in and out. The intention of this hand signal is likely to invite the recipient to *come in* or *come here*. The problem is that the way people beckon one another around the world can be almost as diverse as the way we bid farewell to one another (Axtell 1991, 30).

Making use of nonverbal signals (to go along with words) can indeed be an effective way to communicate with those who don't share the same language. The problem is when we assume that nonverbal gestures carry the same meaning across cultures. In the case at hand, the gesture Caroline used was the same gesture Malaysians use to call a dog. No wonder Haziq was offended!

TIPS FOR COMMUNICATING NONVERBALLY ACROSS DIFFERENCES

- Practice reading between the lines and decoding nonverbal subtleties your clients/partners/employees bring to the conversation.

- Pay attention to the role that social status and nonverbal behavior (i.e., pauses, silences, tone of voice, or roundabout ways of expression) play in the conversation.

- Never project your idea of an appropriate handshake onto others. Likewise, never judge the character or personality of individuals you are dealing with by the nature of their grasp.

- For many of our international partners, although they may understand we are not deliberately trying to offend them, we risk embarrassing them (and ourselves) when using gestures they consider inappropriate.

- As we work with Muslim colleagues or partners, be cognizant of the "left hand" etiquette. Not doing so would be insulting and embarrassing.

- Whenever possible, match your behavior to those of your target culture.

CHAPTER 5

The Difference Between "Me-Focus" And "Group-Focus" Individuals

The United States is the major exporter of modern organization theories, but its position of extreme individualism in comparison to most other countries makes the relevance of some of its theories in other cultural environments doubtful.

—Geert Hofstede

Cultural Incident: The Distribution Of Rewards

You work for a multinational corporation specializing in road construction. The company just won a contract to rehabilitate the road network in Manipur, a state in northeastern India. Despite being one of the poorest states in India (poverty level around 37 percent), Manipur is known for its natural beauty. It is surrounded by nine hills with an oval-shaped valley at the center, thus the nickname *The Jewel of India.*

While the agriculture sector has a vital place in the economy of the state, tourism is becoming a fast-growing industry. This is a problem because the road network of Manipur, which connects all the important cities and distant villages, is in terrible shape. Large stretches are filled with dangerous potholes, the asphalt is deteriorating, and mudslides during the rainy season cause many accidents. Often, medical help does not reach victims of accidents because of the poor road conditions.

You are overseeing a team of six engineers who, after the planning and research phases of the project are completed, will also help, in some capacity, with the construction and maintenance phases of the project. Your company received $3 million for the initial phase of the project. Because of some creative cost-saving measures and hard work, phase one was completed with a $20,000 surplus. As the senior project manager, you decide to distribute these savings among the six team members—mainly because you want to stress the idea that hard work will be rewarded.

Here are the individuals who worked on the project and their levels of contribution.

Arjun: MIT graduate with international experience in Canada and Dubai. He is a hard worker and supervised many day-to-day project operations. You know that at least 40 percent of the work was done by him.

Krishna, Rajesh, and Vijay: Competent but not remarkable workers. Each contributed about 15 percent of the work.

Neil: He comes from a wealthy and well-known family in Manipur. He was not involved with the day-to-day operations of the project (about 5 percent contribution). However, he called upon his connections (his uncle is the governor) and used his influence so that your company was awarded the contract.

Kamal: Hard worker but only contributed 10 percent to the project. He is well-liked but is going through some difficult times. His father just died, and he is now in charge of funding the education of his two young brothers. He is also supporting his mother since his father left no estate.

If you were asked to help decide how the $20,000 should be distributed among the six team members, how much would you give each team member?

The Difference Between Me-Focus/ Individualism And Group-Focus/Collectivism

Hofstede (1980, 1991, 2001) was the first to highlight this cultural difference in his large-scale study of 116,000 managers and employees of a large multinational corporation with subsidiaries in fifty different countries. This dimension has to do with the tendency of society to emphasize the importance of individual identity over group identity, individual rights over group rights, and individual needs over group needs (Ting-Toomey and Chung 2012). In other words, whose goals are more important: those of the individual or those of the group?

Scholars have found that in 70 percent of cultures throughout the world, the needs of the group (i.e., family, community, and organizations) come before those of any one individual (Thiederman 1991). It is also understood that the United States is the world's most individualistic nation (Hofstede 1980).

Individualism

In individualistic societies, such as the United States, an individual's personal goals receive priority consideration over those of the group. In other words, individuals decide what is best for themselves and work toward accomplishing those goals.

Individualists are self-reliant, have more of a sense of separation from their extended family and their community, and work hard to pursue their own goals. In individualistic societies, people are hired, fired, or promoted because of their skills and past achievements. In fact, competence and ability are key factors in hiring and promotion within organizations. Nepotism is frowned upon since it places kinship above competence in hiring and promotion decisions (Brislin 1994).

In the workplace, employees feel compelled to distinguish themselves from others, and unique personal contributions are not only recognized but rewarded (Solomon and Schell 2009). Personal goals come first, and individuals stay with an organization as long as it does not prevent them from meeting their own goals.

Collectivism

Collectivism refers to the broad value tendencies of a culture in emphasizing the importance of *we* over *I*, group rights over individual rights, and group needs over individual needs (Carr-Ruffino 2015).

Collectivists often downplay their own goals in favor of group preferences, and their primary concern is how their decisions will affect others in the group (Brislin 1994). For example, a scholarship offer to pursue graduate studies in another country will only be accepted after consultation with immediate and extended family members and consideration from multiple perspectives (Hsu 1981). The concern: *If I leave the country, how am I going to fulfill my obligations to my family? Will others in the group be able to fulfill those obligations?*

In these cultures, there is a greater sense of involvement in each other's lives, and if you have a problem, you should seek help from the group. For example, if you need a loan, you don't go to a bank; you ask family members first. While individualists would prefer not to burden family members with their problem, collectivists would likely take offense if you didn't.

A collectivist's sense of identity is intricately connected to that of his or her group, be it family or organization. Individuals work hard for the good of the organization because their self-worth is connected to the success of that organization. In fact, the same time, energy, and loyalty given to family is extended to the organization (Triandis, Brislin, and Hui 1988). Members expect the group to look after their interests and concerns throughout their lifetimes. Table 5.1 shows the position of selected cultures in the individualism-collectivism continuum.

TABLE 5.1: Position Of Selected Cultures In The Individualism/Collectivism Continuum

Individualist					Collectivist
USA	UK	Russia	Japan	M. East	SE Asia
	France	India		Mexico	China
	Germany	Spain		Africa	

Adapted from Craig Storti, 1999, Figuring Foreigners Out

How Individualism And Collectivism Play Out In The Workplace

Diversity, globalization, and increased migration bring individuals with different cultural orientations together. Following is a discussion of how individualism and collectivism impact the workplace.

Impact On The Interview Process

Individualism and collectivism play a crucial role in the way individuals present themselves in interviews. While qualified, individualistic candidates have no problem being outspoken and feel comfortable sharing their accomplishments, group-focused, collectivistic candidates feel it would be inappropriate for them to talk about their own accomplishments (Solomon and Schell 2009).

Those involved in the hiring process need to see this for what it is—a cultural difference. Because collectivistic candidates won't freely share what they have done, you need to find creative ways to explore their past accomplishments and skills. One strategy is to tailor your questions in a way that gives the candidate an opportunity to highlight their accomplishments as part of a team and not as an individual.

Impact On Talent Recognition

Individualists expect their efforts to be recognized and are proud to be singled out for their accomplishments. Employee-of-the-month programs, designated parking spaces, additional compensation, and activities commending individual performance are common in individualistic organizations. These types of activities also ensure those being recognized serve as a role model for the rest of the organization.

For collectivists, though, the situation is quite different. The act of singling out an individual, at best, would be embarrassing, and at worst, would confuse and even demoralize the individual and the group (Solomon and Schell 2009, 104). That is because, for these individuals, success is accomplished through cooperation, thus making it inappropriate to single out one individual for praise or recognition. In fact, their belief is that goals are accomplished because of the creative talent of the group and not the capabilities of one outstanding member (Solomon and Schell 2009, 105).

Impact On Decision-Making

In the US, you demonstrate maturity when you are capable of making decisions independently; adults have the autonomy to decide what is best for themselves. In Asia or the Middle East, though, it is in poor form to make a decision on one's own (Thiederman 1991, 119).

The need to consult with others in the group before a decision is made is also prevalent in the workplace. For collectivists, not only must all individuals be consulted, but they all need to be in agreement before a decision is finally made. US business leaders often express frustration with their Asian counterparts because of the ongoing need for meetings to reach a decision (Solomon and Schell 2009). That is because, in these cultures, decisions are not made by a single person. A delegation gathers for a meeting, they deliberate, and then bring the issues to their superiors in the home office. Everyone involved is consulted before the decision is made. In individualistic organizations, though, managers are more inclined to go along with what the majority decided since unanimity is not necessary.

Impact On Competition

In the US, individuals learn about the importance of competition at an early age, and it is highly encouraged, if not expected. In the American workplace, competition encourages efficiency, creativity, product quality, and increased options for customers (Bhashin 2020). In many cultures, though, competition among individual members of a group is disruptive to productivity and harmony.

When working with group-focused employees, managers should be cautious about encouraging competition and singling individuals out since it may have the opposite effect. Instead, promote group pride rather than disrupt the group in the name of individual achievement (Thiederman 1991, 120).

Impact On Goal Achievement

The goals of individuals take precedence in the US. In many other cultures, though, the goals of the group—be it family, company, or even nation—are more important. In fact, the individual who places his or her desires above the group is selfish and inconsiderate (Thiederman 1991, 121).

In the workplace, this cultural difference may play out when employees don't ask for a promotion if they feel their professional advancement will negatively impact group harmony. Thiederman (1991, 121) argues that managers must remember that such an attitude by no means connotes low self-esteem or lack of assertiveness but, instead, reflects an honorable concern for the good of [the] company or business.

Impact On Performance Evaluation

Concern for the group also impacts the way individuals view project success or failure. In this country, we tend to see mistakes as learning opportunities. We also take responsibility for our contribution to a project's success or failure. In collectivistic cultures, however, the group assumes responsibility for successes and failures. That is because it would be inappropriate to call attention to the failures of one individual (Thiederman 1991).

Because of this concern of how the mistake will affect the group, it is not uncommon for group-first individuals to avoid taking the initiative or even voicing their own opinions. In essence, they want to avoid making an error or saying something that would reflect on the abilities of the group as a whole (Thiederman 1991, 117). A favorable group evaluation is imperative, and team members work hard to make sure the reputation of the group remains intact.

If the need arises and you must criticize the performance of a group-focused employee, the culturally competent manager would be wiser to criticize the group as a whole than to pick out the one individual responsible (Thiederman 1991, 120). The same goes for praise. Many group-oriented workers will respond more favorably to praise directed to the entire group than to the delivery of individual compliments.

Table 5.2 provides a detailed summary of the differences between me-focus/individualistic and group-focus/collectivistic societies.

TABLE 5.5: Summary Of The Differences Between Me-Focus/Individualistic And Group-Focus/Collectivistic Societies

Me-Focus	Group-Focus
Individual Characteristics	
Individuals are encouraged to be self-sufficient, to make it on their own, and to think for themselves.	Individuals place priority on the team and the community. Their identity is connected to the group.
Individuals are likely to cut the apron strings when they reach adulthood. In fact, adults are expected to leave home and establish themselves as independent individuals.	Bonds with the parents and grandparents are never severed; they are maintained and reinforced. It is expected that the group will look after their interests and concerns throughout their lifetime.

Individual goals receive priority consideration over those of the group. Individuals decide what is best for them and work toward accomplishing those goals.	The welfare of the group, be it family or organization, is what matters the most; individuals downplay their needs and goals for the welfare of the group.
Respect for individual privacy.	There is a far greater sense of involvement in each other's personal life.
Prefer independent problem-solving.	Prefer group problem-solving since groups maximize ideas that help them reach better solutions.
In The Workplace	
Individual accomplishments are recognized and rewarded.	It is inappropriate to call attention to the achievements or failures of the individual since this would disrupt the harmony of the group.
Decisions are made by an individual or majority vote. Meetings are scheduled to maximize time. Quick decisions are expected.	Decision-making takes much longer since it is imperative that everyone is heard. Many meetings may be necessary to gain group consensus and reach a decision.
People are hired, fired, or promoted because of their skills and past achievements. Competence and ability are key factors in hiring and promotion within organizations. Nepotism is frowned upon.	Nepotism is acceptable since it enforces the notion that kinship takes precedence over competence in hiring and promotion decisions.
Individuals move from job to job in search of a new challenge —even if they are happy and well-compensated in their current position.	Company loyalty is more important. Leaving the organization could disrupt group harmony.
Promotions are based on performance and achievement. High performers are more likely to gain leadership positions.	Promotions are based on seniority and experience, not solely on performance and achievement.

Cultural Incident Revisited

From the road construction cultural incident, we know that people on the team didn't all contribute the same amount to the project. So how should the rewards for the completion of the task be distributed to the engineers? The correct answer is: It depends on whether your value orientation is centered on individualism or collectivism.

Brislin (1994) argues that individualists tend to favor an equitable distribution of rewards. That is, rewards should be distributed based on a person's contribution. Because of that, individualists would likely distribute the reward based on individual contributions (40 percent, 15 percent each to three employees, 10 percent, and 5 percent).

Individualists also believe in rewarding hard work and individual accomplishments. Not doing so would give individuals less of an incentive to work hard and strive to be their best. What would be the point of working hard if there were no rewards to be gained? The reward doesn't necessarily need to be in the form of financial compensation; it could be an award or a mention in the company newsletter. The point is that individuals expect to be recognized for their efforts.

For collectivists, on the other hand, equality is more important. Everyone receives the same level of reward, regardless of their level of contribution. It does not matter that Arjun was the one who carried the project to completion. For collectivists, the group matters more than a single individual. The cohesiveness of the group is more important than singling out one or two individuals. Awarding one individual more than the others could disrupt group cohesiveness.

Collectivists are also more involved in each other's lives. This would compel them to ensure Kamal receives additional funding because of the difficult family situation he is facing. He did not contribute as much to the project, but the group understands why and feels it is necessary to help him during difficult times. The individual is cared for and protected by the group.

TIPS FOR WORKING WITH GROUP-FOCUS/ COLLECTIVISTIC WORKERS

- Collectivists or group-focused candidates won't freely list their accomplishments. During the hiring process, tailor your questions to give the candidate an opportunity to highlight his/ her accomplishments while they were part of a team.

- Singling out individuals for their accomplishments would likely embarrass them. In such situations, praise the group and not the individual.

- In decision-making, remember that all individuals need to be in agreement before a choice is made.

- Competition among individual members of a group is disruptive to productivity as well as to group harmony.

- Workers will not ask for a promotion if they feel their professional advancement will negatively impact group harmony. This attitude by no means connotes low self-esteem or lack of assertiveness but, instead, reflects an honorable concern for the good of the team.

- It is not uncommon for group-focus individuals to avoid taking initiative or even voicing their own opinions. This comes from concern in making a mistake or saying something that would impact the group as a whole in a negative way.

- It is important that you learn to become emotionally involved with group-focus coworkers or employees.

CHAPTER 6

Power Distance: Not Everyone Is Created Equal

The hierarchical nature of Indian society demands that there is a boss and that the boss should be seen to be the boss. Everyone else just does as they are told, and even if they know the boss is 100 percent wrong, no one will argue.

—Gitanjali Kolanad

Cultural Incident: Big Box Failure**

Walmart is considered the world's largest brick-and-mortar retailer. In fact, for its 2017 fiscal year, the company reported worldwide sales revenue of almost $375 billion. Currently, it operates over 11,000 stores in twenty-seven different countries.

In the 1990s, Walmart began branching out internationally. According to a report published by the Institute for World Economics and International Management (Knorr and Arndt 2003), Walmart initiated the process of opening stores in Germany in 1997. The goal was to implement the same management, marketing, and customer service philosophy in Germany that had proven immensely successful in the United States. That is, keep it informal, friendly, and egalitarian.

Germany was an obvious choice because it was one of the world's largest economies at the time. It also had a relatively affluent population, with most of them having a good command of English, which would facilitate the adoption of Walmart's corporate culture efficiently. Lastly, Germans were already familiar with stores like Walmart since they had embraced two of its competitors.

To run Walmart's German operation, an individual who had successfully managed 200 Walmart stores in the United States was chosen. He did not speak German, which led to him requiring all German store managers to speak English at work.

The process began with Walmart purchasing existing retail operations from Wertkauf, a chain of supermarkets with a wide assortment of nonfood goods similar to Walmart in the United States. It also purchased operations from Spar Handels, which operated grocery wholesale and retail stores. In essence, Walmart was able to acquire not only an existing workforce but also their complete operating facilities, which allowed them to open eighty-five stores throughout Germany. The thinking was that to make those old stores into Walmart stores, all they needed was employees with the right uniform and some training in the company's friendly and helpful customer service style.

However, in 2006, Walmart announced it was closing its German operations, with $1 billion in losses. This happened close to the company's exit from South Korea. Zimmerman and Nelson (2006) contend that beyond the huge monetary loss, this was also a huge strategic failure because, had it been successful, Walmart would have been able to enter other parts of Europe and be in a better position to negotiate with local suppliers.

What brought the giant store down? Did cultural differences play a role in their demise?

***Adapted from Solomon and Schell 2009 and Knorr and Arndt 2003*

Are We All Really Created Equal?

In most Western cultures, the belief is that all individuals are created equal. Because of that, they should all have equal opportunities to advance in life. Other cultures, though, accept the idea that some people are naturally more powerful, affluent, and advantaged than others

(Carr-Ruffino 2015, 47), and power should not be distributed equally among its members. In fact, the expectation is that there should be a greater power distance among members.

Power distance refers to how much equality or inequality people within a particular society accept or expect (Bucher 2008, 235). In some societies, you will find a large power distance among its members, while in others, that power distance will be much smaller.

Large Power Distance

In larger power distance societies, inequality is expected. In the workplace, this translates into centralized decision-making, followed by clear orders on how those decisions should be carried out. Leaders sit at the top of the organizational chart (more like a pyramid) and rarely seek input from employees since this would likely be seen as a sign of weakness (Carr-Ruffino 2015). Likewise, it would be highly inappropriate for a supervisor to pitch in and help during crunch time.

In these societies, employees do not expect to be consulted. They follow orders and would never argue a point with their superiors, nor would they point out a problem with their leader's decision. To them, bosses do the bossing and employees do the work, and deviations from that norm imply that one or the other can't do their jobs properly (Carr-Ruffino 2015, 48). There is a lot more deference for those in power, and relationships between employees and supervisors are kept formal and impersonal (Hofstede 1980).

Small Power Distance

Those coming from small power distance societies, on the other hand, believe everyone should have an equal opportunity to succeed, and all individuals should be equally respected. Meritocracy is a value which leads to the assumption that the best and the brightest will be rewarded.

Employees in small power distance organizations are independent, feel free to express themselves, and may even question those in power. They feel empowered to make decisions and take action and expect to be consulted, especially if decisions will impact them. Their role is to see a task to completion and not simply follow instructions. The organizational chart is flatter, and decision-making is decentralized. The belief is that power lies in the role, not in the superiority of a person (Carr-Ruffino 2015). In these societies, employees tend to see their superiors more like their equal. It is quite common for employees and their superiors to socialize, and their relationships may be more personable. Pulling rank on this group would not be appropriate. Table 6.1 shows where countries sit in the high/low power distance continuum.

TABLE 6.1: Country Distribution In The Large/ Small Power Distance Continuum

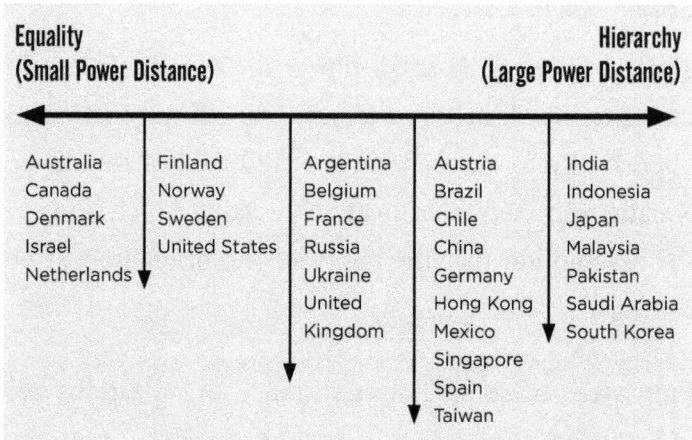

Equality (Small Power Distance) ← → **Hierarchy (Large Power Distance)**

Australia	Finland	Argentina	Austria	India
Canada	Norway	Belgium	Brazil	Indonesia
Denmark	Sweden	France	Chile	Japan
Israel	United States	Russia	China	Malaysia
Netherlands		Ukraine	Germany	Pakistan
		United Kingdom	Hong Kong	Saudi Arabia
			Mexico	South Korea
			Singapore	
			Spain	
			Taiwan	

Adapted from Solomon and Schell 2009, Managing Across Cultures: The Seven Keys To Doing Business With A Global Mindset.

The Impact Of Power Distance In The Workplace

Experts argue that if you are working in a multicultural environment or are doing business in the global marketplace, power distance is a dimension you need to understand because it is fundamental to the success of a business endeavor (Solomon and Schell 2009, 82). This cultural dimension impacts several aspects of the workplace; some of them will be discussed in the paragraphs that follow.

Leadership Style

Power distance impacts the way individuals lead their organizations. In fact, leadership style varies a great deal between large power distance and small power distance societies. In small power distance—more egalitarian—societies, leaders ask their employees for input rather than issuing directives. In fact, good leaders are those who seek input from the team. There is a general sense that anyone is capable of achieving a leadership position as long as they aspire to it and demonstrate they have the skills to perform the job. In large power distance—more hierarchical—societies, leadership positions tend to be assigned to the oldest person or the one with the longest tenure.

Decision-Making

This dimension also impacts who is empowered to make decisions in the organization. In more egalitarian societies, employees tend to participate in the decision-making process. Once a decision is agreed upon, the team is then responsible for executing it. In hierarchical societies (large power distance), team members expect direction. Decisions are made by leaders who often do not seek input from their employees. In fact, a supervisor who seeks input or leaves decisions up to the employees would be considered weak and would lose face with his employees. In some circumstances, such as in a meeting, it is not uncommon for employees to defer their decisions to the most senior person in the room even if they are capable of participating in the process.

Meeting Behaviors

Meetings are conducted differently between the two groups. In large power distance societies, meetings are conducted for relaying decisions that have already been made or will be made by the leader. In addition:

> *[I] it is considered embarrassing and inappropriate to ask subordinates for their opinion in the presence of senior managers. Time and again, we hear stories about Chinese, Indian, and Japanese workers who won't speak during a meeting because someone of higher status is present. (Solomon and Schell 2009, 88)*

In small power distance societies, employees are encouraged, even expected, to participate and speak up during meetings, regardless of who else is present.

Age Difference

Age difference is also a factor that needs to be considered. In hierarchical, large power distance societies, age is likely a prerequisite for achieving a leadership position. In more egalitarian (small power distance) societies such as the US, age is unrelated to advancement. This may pose a challenge in situations where a younger manager is supervising an older employee with a more hierarchical orientation. It is not uncommon for immigrants and international business people to question decisions recommended by those who are younger. In customer service situations and even negotiations, younger individuals are at a disadvantage since they are perceived as having no decision-making power (Thiederman 1991). In these situations, ensuring they do have the backing and full support of their leaders would facilitate the process.

Gender

Gender may also impact success or failure in negotiations or in the work environment. In this country, it is possible to find women in leadership positions. This is less likely (though not impossible) in large power distance societies. Just like being young, women may be ignored and are assumed to lack the authority to make decisions. If that is the case, Thiederman (1991) suggests finding the *informal leader* of the group and working closely through that individual. The key is for women in leadership positions to show respect for male workers without ever conceding their position of authority.

Meeting Deadlines

In this country, it is not unheard of for supervisors to step in in order to meet a fast-approaching deadline. For those with a more hierarchical inclination, though, this can be seen as a sign of weakness on the part of the supervisor. This type of behavior may also be construed as the supervisor feeling the employees are not doing their job properly. In this situation, it is important that you make sure your large power distance employees see your help as a way to get the job done by the expected deadline and not a reflection on their performance.

What To Expect When Working Across These Two Dimensions

In *Managing Across Cultures: The Seven Keys To Doing Business With A Global Mindset*, Solomon and Schell (2009) suggest that when working with more egalitarian, low power distance individuals, it is important to keep the following in mind:

- Less hierarchy is better. Informality in the relationship is preferred despite differences in status.

- Employees expect to be treated as equals and to participate in the decision-making process. They speak up in meetings and provide ideas or unsolicited opinions.

- Status symbols are less important and considered pompous. Leaders and employees may address each other by their first name.

- Supervisors empower their employees to make their own decisions.

- During meetings, employees are encouraged to speak up regardless of who else is present.

- Men and women are treated basically in the same way.

They also suggest keeping in mind the following when working with more hierarchical, high power distance individuals:

- Status and social class are important. People are not equal, and there needs to be a formal relationship between individuals with different social statuses.

- Leaders are responsible for making decisions. Asking for input from subordinates makes them look ineffective and diminishes their credibility.

- Signs of power and position (i.e., car model, stylish clothes, office size) are important because they convey authority. Leaders are addressed by their titles and/or last name.

Empowering employees can be disruptive:

- Individuals expect direction from their leaders and do not challenge the opinions of those who are in power.
- Meetings are held with individuals of similar rank and positions. If subordinates join the meeting, they are not expected to participate.

Revisiting The Cultural Incident

So, what brought Walmart down? Experts agree that a great deal of Walmart's failure was indeed due to its inability to account for cultural differences—and there were many.

The first roadblock to Walmart's success was the smiling greeters. Solomon and Schell (2009) argue that Germany is a formal, hierarchical society. Smiles are only reserved for people they know; in other words, their friends. Greeting customers with a smile works well in the United States, which tends to be more egalitarian and values informality. In Germany, the greeters were seen as intrusive and presumptuous. No wonder many of the women walking into a Walmart in Germany thought the greeters were flirting with them. In addition, the practice of employees helping customers locate what they needed was often seen as harassment.

In Walmart stores in the United States, a common practice is that each morning, employees would gather to chant "W-A-L-M-A-R-T," usually led by local leaders. For the German employees, this early-morning merriment was downright embarrassing. Seeing their leaders, whom they held with great respect and deference, in such a degrading role, was not acceptable. Germany is more hierarchical than the United States; leaders are expected to demonstrate leadership in an *upward connection*, not a downward one (Solomon and Schell 2009). Socializing with the general employee population is frowned upon. Leaders are expected to be formal, dress in a more upscale way, and even act in ways that show power and authority. Clearly, the cheers were not appropriate for the German workplace. More distressing was the fact that it put their leaders in a role that employees deemed as demeaning and embarrassing.

The bottom line: just because employees switched their usual uniforms for the Walmart apron, it did not mean their cultural values switched as well. Knorr and Arndt (2003) argued that the German's attitudes toward hierarchy and egalitarianism did, in fact, play a big role in Walmart's demise in Germany.

TIPS FOR WORKING WITH LARGE POWER DISTANCE, MORE HIERARCHICAL WORKERS

- Formality, respect, deference, titles, and chain of command are important for these individuals. In some places, such as India, ranking is determined at birth.

- These employees are less likely to raise questions; it is important to check for understanding frequently. While you may see this as micromanaging, they will likely interpret this behavior as a sign of good leadership on your part.

- You will put them in a difficult position by expecting an immediate answer, especially during negotiations. Because of their strong sense of hierarchy, there will likely be a lot of consultation with their superiors before an answer is given. Insisting on an answer will likely get you either silence or false promises in return.

- You can still encourage participation in decision-making and maintain their respect. You accomplish that by making clear that while you are seeking their input, the final decision will indeed be yours.

CHAPTER 7

Tolerance Or Intolerance For Change

The chameleon does not leave one tree until he is sure of another.

—Saudi Arabian proverb

Cultural Incident: How Much Risk Should Be Tolerated?**

The British division of a major oil and gas company was in the process of identifying exploration locations in the Persian Gulf. Given that many sites were promising, the company decided to establish a strategic partnership with a similar company in Houston, Texas, in the United States.

Houston is considered the oil capital of the US. Some go as far as calling it the energy capital of the *world*. Every segment of the energy industry, including exploration, production, transmission, marketing, supply, and technology, is located in Houston. The city is home to forty-four of the nation's 128 publicly-traded oil and gas exploration and production companies. One-third of this nation's jobs related to oil and gas extraction is located in Houston, and the city is also at the center stage of most foreign investment in energy. In theory, the partnership between the British and the Americans had everything going for it.

While the British were taking the lead, major decisions still had to be approved by the company in Houston. Much to the British division's consternation, though, every proposal submitted had been rejected. The British were at a loss since the proposals were being written by the top exploration engineers in Europe. Furthermore, preliminary tests had indeed indicated the sites they identified were worthy of further exploration. Senior members of the British team were convinced this was due to a communication breakdown.

Getting the two teams physically together seemed to be a logical next step. However, this did not improve the situation at all. The Americans, with their go-get-them attitude, were often put off by what they perceived as the persistent gloom-and-doom attitude of their British colleagues. Their need to rehash in great detail everything that could possibly go wrong with the project only served to dampen the creativity and, ultimately, the productivity of the Americans. Their last meeting deteriorated to the point where the Americans decided to cut short what was supposed to be a three-day meeting. Back in the US, the team reported to their senior leadership that they saw no future for this project due to the negativity of their interactions.

As a last-ditch effort, both the Houston and British leadership decided to examine what seemed to be the source of the problem. What could possibly bring mature and highly competent engineers to this level of frustration? Were there any cultural barriers at play?

** *Adapted from Solomon and Schell 2009*

How Groups Differ In Their Tolerance (Or Intolerance) For Change

There is no denying that some individuals are more comfortable in dealing with risk, change, and uncertainty than others. This is as much as a personality trait, as it is a cultural difference. While some cultural differences are easy to recognize, for example, how a group perceives the role of an authority figure (as discussed in Chapter 6), others, such as tolerance for change, are not. In fact, Schell and Dubberke (2018) argue that this cultural difference is one of the more subtle and hardest to recognize.

Change tolerance refers to attitudes toward newness, embracing different ways of doing things, and whether or not individuals view change as bringing opportunity or threat (Schell and Dubberke 2018). Some groups tend to see change as a positive force, while others tend to be more change-averse; they lean toward avoiding uncertainty and ambiguity.

Hofstede, Hofstede, and Minkov (2010) developed the *uncertainty avoidance* (UA) index. This index measures whether individuals in a society have a high or low tolerance for uncertainty and ambiguity. In other words, it shows the extent to which members of a culture are comfortable dealing with uncertain situations or if their tendency is to avoid those types of situations. The former are comfortable with risk-taking, change, and innovation. The latter, needless to say, have a greater need for predictability, structure, and rules. Cultures can score high or low in the UA index.

Cultures that score high in the UA index like to play it safe (Hofstede 1984). They have a low tolerance for change, uncertainty, ambiguity, and risk-taking, so they try to control or avoid uncertainty by putting strict rules and regulations in place. For these groups, change brings about unknowns and uncertainties, and, for them, the best way to deal with those uncertainties is to stick to tradition. There are formal rules and standards, and people know what is expected of them. Deviation from these rules and standards is considered disruptive. In these societies, individuals tend to avoid conflict, seek consensus, and take fewer risks (Gill 2017) since failure is something to be ashamed of even when it brings with it valuable lessons (Solomon and Schell 2009, 191).

Cultures that score low on the UA index tend to have a high tolerance for change, uncertainty, ambiguity, and risk-taking. *Nothing ventured, nothing gained* is their motto. Individuals see change as necessary and accept it as such. Flexibility and tolerance toward divergent opinions and behaviors are also common in these cultures (Belyh 2019). Table 7.1 shows examples of high- and low-UA cultures.

TABLE 7.1: Examples Of High And Low Uncertainty Avoidance Cultures

Higher UA Countries Change Averse Lower Risk-Takers	**Lower UA Countries** Change Tolerant Higher Risk-Takers
Greece	United States
Italy	India
Mexico	China
South Korea	Indonesia
Belgium	Singapore
Russia	Sweden

The Impact On Organizations

Play-it-safe organizations, also referred to as change-averse organizations, control risk-taking by enforcing strict and clearly outlined approval systems. Consequently, young employees do not present bold, new concepts and tend to leave the decision-making to older and more senior managers (Solomon and Schell 2009, 191).

Scholars (Solomon and Schell 2009; Belyh 2019; Schell and Dubberke 2018) have found that organizations in high-UA cultures tend to:

- Avoid risk and ambiguity; in fact, new ideas tend to be met with resistance ("We have always done it this way; why change it now?").
- See change as a threat to tradition.
- Have standardized procedures, written rules and regulations, and clearly defined processes.
- Require consensus prior to decision-making.
- Insist on detailed planning with minimal tolerance for deviations.
- Avoid failure at all costs; thus, the need to consider everything that could go wrong.

- Promote employees based on age and seniority.
- Place a high value on employees' loyalty to the organization.

Low-UA organizations, on the other hand, are more tolerant of change and view uncertainty and ambiguity as natural and necessary. They value creativity, encourage individual choice, and employees are encouraged to take risks (Gill 2017; Adler 2008). Their structures are more flexible, employees feel comfortable in providing input to colleagues and supervisors, and leaders are expected to be change agents and visionaries (Solomon and Schell 2009).

In these organizations, there is a higher tolerance for failure as long as you learn from the experience. Rules have their place, but there are exceptions to every rule, and an organization's success is dependent on individuals coming up with new ways of doing things such as developing new products, new types of services, and new technology. These organizations tend to be more forward-looking as the expectation is that they will, eventually, reap the benefits from their investment (Hofstede 1984).

Research (Solomon and Schell 2009; Schell and Dubberke 2018) shows that organizations in low-UA cultures:

- Have a higher tolerance for ambiguity and risk-taking.
- See change as positive because it can bring about innovation.
- Place a high value on creativity; there are always new ways of doing things.
- Develop broad plans and project guidelines that focus on achieving expected goals but do not necessarily establish how individuals should get there. Autonomy and flexibility are expected.
- Failure is seen as a learning opportunity.
- There is more employee turnover; employees see change as a positive step in their own careers.
- Loyalty to the organization is not as highly valued.

Cultural Incident Revisited

At first glance, we are inclined to think that the British and the Americans are not that far apart, culturally speaking. As you will see, this is a dangerous assumption to make.

According to Solomon and Schell (2009), one of the main reasons for their disagreement had to do with how the groups looked at risk-taking. US Americans tend to be a lot more risk-tolerant than the British. In fact, in the US, failures do serve a purpose as long as we learn from our mistakes.

The biggest discord between the two groups was approaching the project from two different angles. One was looking at all the risks, while the other was focusing on the potential to succeed. For the British, it was essential to list all the possible risks followed by detailed discussions of how these risks would impact the project. The Americans, on the other hand, preferred a different approach. Despite recognizing the potential risks, focusing on the potential for success was more important.

The British assumed the Americans did not take the project's risks seriously, were inappropriately optimistic, and were careless in funding high-risk projects. The Americans, in contrast, assumed the British were unnecessarily negative and acted as if failure was a given. This led them to assume the British were not as vested in the successful completion of the project (Solomon and Schell 2009).

Clearly, both groups needed a better understanding of each other's cultural perceptions related to risk tolerance or aversion. Risk-tolerant cultures tend to look at projects as potential opportunities for growth, and ultimately, success. If the project fails, it serves as a valuable learning opportunity. As the US adage goes, "If at first you don't succeed, try, try again."

Risk-averse cultures, on the other hand, implement changes only after all the potential pitfalls have been considered and analyzed in full. That is because risky opportunities carry the potential for failure; failure is embarrassing and should be avoided at all costs.

TIPS FOR WORKING WITH CHANGE-AVERSE/RISK-AVERSE WORKERS

- Don't expect employees to accept change easily. You will likely meet less resistance if you build support for the new procedures you plan to implement. In fact, plan on providing more detail and rationale to support the need for the project. Expect it will likely take longer for the implementation to take place.

- In performance evaluations, remember the expectation that employees assume they will remain with the company for life or for much of their career. Poor performance needs to be dealt with in a way that is culturally appropriate. Be sensitive to the employee's age and longevity in the company.

- To avoid stress and anxiety, make sure you have standardized procedures, written rules and regulations, and clearly defined processes in place.

- Understand that, from these employees' perspective, rules are not to be broken.

- In decision-making, remember the need for consensus.

PART III

Next Steps: Sustaining A Diverse And Inclusive Global Organization

CHAPTER 8

How Biases Impact Diversity And Inclusion

But I think that, no matter how smart, people usually see what they're already looking for, that's all.

—Veronica Roth, Allegiant

Which (If Any) Of These Individuals Are Guilty Of Bias?

Situation 1. Mary Ellen, a manager at Dermatology Consultants, had just finished interviewing the finalists for an entry-level IT position. Kevin, who was in his mid-twenties, was her top choice. In a meeting with the search committee, she expressed her concerns. She wanted to offer Kevin the position, but she was worried about his long-term commitment to the company. Data shows individuals in Kevin's age bracket do tend to change jobs more often than others. Indeed, a glance at Kevin's resume shows he had changed jobs three times since graduating from college. Is Mary Ellen being biased toward Kevin?

Situation 2. Henry tried to listen attentively as Zhang Wei, a new addition to the engineering division, presented his design idea. The problem was that Zhang Wei spoke with a heavy accent, which made comprehension difficult. During the presentation, Henry mostly nodded and maintained as much eye contact as he deemed appropriate and tried to show interest. The reality was that he understood little of what was being presented. However, because he knew all the Asians in the company were superb engineers, he felt it would be best not to make Zhan Wei lose face by disclosing his poor understanding of Zhang Wei's concepts. Is Henry guilty of bias?

The Difference Between Stereotypes, Biases, And Discrimination

Stereotypes reflect the way we think, biases or prejudices echo the way we feel, and discrimination is the end result of our biased thinking (Carr-Ruffino 2015). As depicted in Figure 8.1, stereotypical thinking may lead to bias as well as discrimination.

FIGURE 8.1: The Pathway From Stereotypes To Discrimination

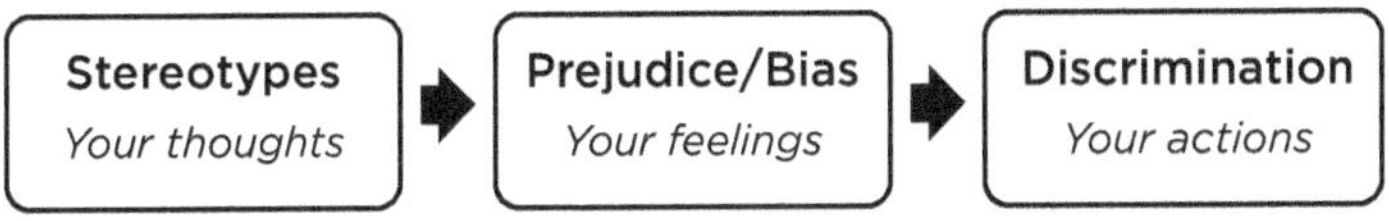

Stereotypes

Every day, our brain is bombarded with millions of bits of information. To make all this information more manageable, we create categories and give them recognizable labels. We try to fit any new information into our existing categories. Whenever we encounter behavior that matches our categories, it reinforces the stereotype. Whenever a behavior disproves the stereotype, though, our tendency is to think of it as an exception to the rule.

Because stereotypes are inflexible generalizations about all individuals of a certain group (i.e., Asians are good in math), they lead us to make assumptions about individuals without taking their unique qualifications into consideration. For example, a hiring manager may bypass an Asian American for a leadership position because of his association of Asians with technical skills rather than leadership skills.

Prejudice Or Bias

Dictionary.com defines bias as a prejudice in favor of or against one thing, person, or group. Prejudice occurs when you judge a whole category of people as basically better or worse than others (Carr-Ruffino 2015, 109), prejudging individuals without really knowing them. In fact, studies show that bias is the biggest advancement barrier women and African American executives face today (Carr-Ruffino 2015; Catalyst 2004). When acted out, prejudice leads to discrimination.

Discrimination

Discrimination is composed of all the actions or practices that result in members of a less-powerful group being treated differently in ways that disadvantage them (Carr-Ruffino 2015, 109). Power differential is essential to perpetuate discrimination, with individuals from historically disadvantaged groups being impacted the most. Discrimination isn't always overt. This is the reason why women and applicants with African American-sounding names still receive fewer job callbacks, lower salary offers, and lower competency rankings (Moss-Racusin, Dovidio, Brescoll, Graham, and Handelsman 2012).

Discrimination is not limited to the workplace, either. Because of COVID-19, for example, Asian Americans are experiencing a surge of verbal and physical assault. Asian

Americans are afraid of grocery shopping, taking mass transportation alone, and even letting their children play outside. This increase in anti-Asian sentiment reflects the growing tendency of blaming Asians for the pandemic.

It is important to keep in mind that, while we cannot prove someone is biased or prejudiced, we can prove when someone's action excludes or disadvantages another person. In fact, civil rights laws have been somewhat effective in offsetting workplace discrimination.

A Deeper Look Into Our Biases

There are multiple ways biases are acquired. Sometimes, we learn them from our parents when they make racist comments. Other times, one negative experience is enough to taint our assumptions toward an entire group. For example, a manager may be hesitant to hire Latinos after a painful divorce from her Latino husband of fifteen years. The media also plays a big role in disseminating biases. After Hurricane Katrina—the costliest tropical cyclone on record—Black residents in New Orleans were often depicted as looting grocery stores while white residents, photographed in the exact same situation, were described as individuals who were trying to find food.

Researchers behind the Implicit Association Test (IAT) have confirmed that we are all biased, whether we admit it or not. Dreasher (2017) has also argued that (1) we all tend to prejudge individuals based on the groups to which they belong, (2) this prejudgment can be positive or negative, and (3) it is virtually impossible to get rid of our tendency to make these prejudgments. Needless to say, these prejudgments prevent us from seeing employees and potential candidates for who they really are, which, in turn, undermines our ability to create diverse, fair, and equitable workplaces.

Most worrisome is the fact that more often than not, we make decisions that impact individuals negatively without any awareness we are being biased. In a study conducted by Bertrand and Mullainathan (2004), researchers confirmed that even names could unconsciously impact people's decision-making. For this study, they distributed 5,000 resumes to over 1,200 employers who were not only hiring but also aggressively trying to diversify their organizations. Some of the resumes had typically white names while others had typically Black ones. Every company was sent four resumes: one of each race that was considered an average resume and one of each race that depicted the individuals as highly skilled. Results showed that candidates with typically white names received 50 percent more callbacks than those with typically Black names. In addition, the average typically white-named candidates received more callbacks than the highly skilled typically Black-named candidates.

It is also worth mentioning that most of the decisions we make are made in a way that confirms the beliefs we already have. Bucher (2008) calls this phenomenon *confirmational behavior*, and, here again, we are unaware it is happening. For example, if I believe in an employee's capacity to succeed, perhaps because she reminds me of myself, I will likely do whatever I can to make sure she succeeds. That is, I will make sure she is on the right track to move up in the company and that she is connected to the people and other resources she needs. With all this support behind her, this employee will, no doubt, thrive in the company, thus confirming my initial belief. Our thoughts and decisions are constantly influenced by our unconscious biases.

The Cost Of Bias And Its Impact In The Workplace

Needless to say, organizations can also be biased. The Corporate Leavers Survey, a national study conducted by the Level Playing Field Institute (2007), shows that each year, more than two million professionals voluntarily leave their jobs solely due to unfair treatment they received because of their race, gender, or sexual orientation. The cost of this turnover is a staggering $64 billion per year.

The cost of unconscious bias is more than attrition, though. Other ways biases compromise success in the workplace include litigation, image loss, inability to relate with diverse customers, increased conflict, and diminished sales. In regards to the latter, the 2019 Multicultural Economy Report revealed that the combined buying power of Blacks, Asian Americans, Native Americans, and Hispanics is estimated to be about $3.9 trillion. Similarly, the buying power of the LGBTQ+ community is $3.7 trillion (Wolny 2019). If organizations do not take steps to address their biases so they can work more effectively with diverse clients, they will, no doubt, shortchange their profits.

The challenge: How do we openly address something that is happening out of most people's awareness? First, we need to recognize we are all biased. Second, we need to do the hard work of understanding how our biases affect our way of thinking, behaving, and functioning. Only then will we be able to mitigate their impact in the workplace. Figure 8.2 depicts a possible pathway for recognizing and eliminating unconscious biases.

Thiederman (2003) contends that biases are like secret beliefs of how we feel about certain groups. Acknowledging our biases, even if just to ourselves, is hard. After all, who wants to be labeled a racist, a sexist, or a homophobe? However, dealing with our biases is essential because it allows us to monitor our thinking, make fewer assumptions, treat employees as individuals, and ultimately, lead more inclusively.

FIGURE 8.2: Pathway To Recognizing And Eliminating Biases

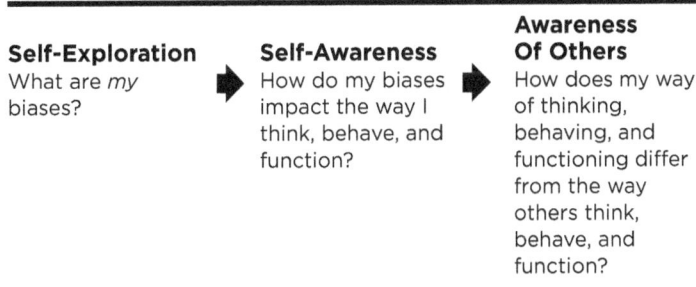

Self-Exploration		**Self-Awareness**		**Awareness Of Others**
What are *my* biases?	→	How do my biases impact the way I think, behave, and function?	→	How does my way of thinking, behaving, and functioning differ from the way others think, behave, and function?

Adapted from Dreasher 2018

If organizations are striving for a diverse workforce, it is essential that hiring managers and individuals on hiring committees understand the role their biases play in hindering this process. In the publication *Proven Strategies for Addressing Unconscious Bias in the Workplace* (Diversity Best Practices 2008, 16), the argument is made that an understanding of unconscious bias is an invitation to a new level of engagement about diversity issues. It requires awareness, introspection, authenticity, humility, and compassion. And most of all, it requires communication and a willingness to act.

Revisiting The Situations

Is Mary Ellen Biased?

No. In addition to current employment data about millennials, Kevin's resume did show he had changed jobs three times since graduation. This is a fact that could be easily verified in his resume. An inflexible belief or assumption about millennials would likely have prevented her from bringing Kevin in for an interview. If this had been the case, Mary Ellen would indeed have been guilty of bias.

Is Henry Biased?

Yes. Clearly, his heart was in the right place. However, his actions only served to exacerbate the problem. First, he led Zhang Wei to believe he understood his concepts, when, in reality, he did not. While he was trying to get around an embarrassing situation for both of them, this could ultimately be costly to the company—not only in terms of wasted time and resources but also in terms of health and safety for potential clients. Second, he assumed Zhang Wei was a good engineer because he was Asian. This is an inflexible, albeit positive, belief and should not be applied to all individuals in the group. Third, he did nothing to address Zhang Wei's communication barrier, thus holding him to a lower standard of excellence. Bias concealed in kindness is still bias.

TIPS FOR LESSENING THE IMPACT OF BIASES IN THE WORKPLACE

- Remember that biases impact our ability to manage and lead effectively.

- No one is born biased; we learn it. As such, biases can be unlearned.

- Self-awareness is key. Lack of awareness of personal biases makes it difficult to manage, unlearn, and accept responsibility for our actions.

- It is important to conduct an audit of company policies and practices for hidden biases in the way you screen and interview candidates, performance evaluations, distribution of resources, opportunities for professional development, etc.

- Survey current and former employees to address the impact of unconscious bias in the organization. Bias training is needed; even though we have laws in place to prevent discrimination based on certain identity characteristics, discrimination still persists. While laws exist to prevent overt acts of discrimination, it is impossible to legislate attitudes.

- Ensuring search committees are properly trained to bring diversity in can enhance the search process. It is important to hold trainings on valuing diversity, developing cultural competence skills, and understanding the impact of unconscious bias in candidate selection.

- Looking for individuals to *fit* into your organization is a poor recruitment strategy; it may be an indication that unconscious bias is at play.

CHAPTER 9

Skills To Work Effectively Across Differences

Leaders who encounter employees or customers behaving in unfamiliar ways need to understand the why behind the behavior.

—Gundling and Williams

In the book *Inclusive Leadership: From Awareness to Action*, Gundling and Williams (2019), the authors describe the conundrum faced by the director of leadership development for a major global organization. The firm had an assessment process that all candidates aspiring to move up in the company had to undergo. The problem was that all Brazilian candidates, even those who were highly qualified, were only passing the test at a 20 percent rate, which was considerably lower than the 50 percent rate of their US peers. While sitting in some of the assessments, she observed:

> *[W]hen the candidates from Brazil were asked a question, they would usually respond first with a story, and only later with an answer. It turned out that they felt this was a better way to get their point across, that was also quite common in their country, but it earned them consistently low grades from our North American assessors. (Gundling and Williams, 2019, 212)*

Clearly, the problem was due to a cultural difference. In fact, the Brazilians were being penalized for lack of clear and direct communication, a typical US communication style. The solution, then, was to coach the Brazilian candidates so they could switch their communication style. Once they were able to shift their cultural perspective and started answering the questions in a more direct way—before telling a story—their scores improved a great deal. The fact that the US group did not recognize the Brazilians' performance as a cultural difference and not a matter of competence speaks to the fact that training is a two-way street. In fact, Dreasher (2017) argues that recognizing and learning about differences will not only strengthen a manager's effectiveness but will also communicate respect for diverse employees. The more managers learn about other cultures and value orientations, the more comfortable they will be around diversity. This, in turn, will increase their readiness to invite more diversity into the organization.

The Skills To Work Effectively Across Cultural Differences

In a global organization, knowledge of cultural differences is key. Without that, leaders and team members may, albeit inadvertently, impose their cultural orientation onto others. For example, when a manager says during a presentation, "Feel free to jump in any time with your questions or concerns," those who share his cultural orientation will interpret that as an open invitation to speak freely and contribute to the discussion. However, those employees who do not share the same cultural orientation would behave quite differently. In Chapter 6, I discussed the concept of power distance. Individuals with large power distance orientation would not expect to be consulted and would never argue a point with a supervisor. Moreover, they would not point out a problem with their leader's proposition, even if they saw one. Leaders should not seek input from these employees since this would likely be seen as a sign of weakness (Carr-Ruffino 2015). A culturally competent leader (as discussed below) is able to recognize how his approach differs from those on his team and incorporates processes that allow all team members to contribute, such as requesting comments not only in person but also in private or via email.

Spitzberg and Changnon (2009, 6) equate competence with a set of abilities or skills; as the process of managing interaction in ways that are likely to produce more appropriate and effective outcomes. Dreasher (2010) argues that culturally competent leaders are those who are a) self-aware, b) knowledgeable of others, and c) have the skills to be able to adjust their behavior to the cultural orientation of others, be it nationality, race, ethnicity, religion, ability, sexual orientation, or any other aspect of their identity. These three steps are discussed below.

Step 1: Develop Self-Awareness

The path to cultural competence starts within. That is, you start by identifying your own personal biases, beliefs, values, stereotypes, prejudices, and privileges (in age, physical ability, education level, sexual orientation, language, etc.). This process will help you understand how these personal characteristics affect your thinking and behavior. By starting this process internally, you begin to recognize that your own perspective is not the only one (or necessarily the most valid one), which will allow the acceptance of different perspectives.

Self-exploration leads to increased self-awareness, an essential element in the understanding of others. Training programs designed to help employees increase their self-awareness should provide opportunities for reflection and discussion on such topics as:

a. How can being a member of a privileged group (e.g., white, male, heterosexual) impact your relationship with employees or clients from a non-privileged group? Or vice versa?

b. How does race, ethnicity, gender, age, religion, sexual orientation, ability, economic class, language, national origin, and so forth impact your interactions with employees or clients?

c. Have you ever been in a situation where you were a minority (outnumbered)? How did you feel? Can you empathize with employees who are from underrepresented populations?

d. What opinions or images do you carry about individuals from [name group]? Are they positive or negative? How did you acquire them? Through personal history? Childhood memories? The media? What steps can you take to eliminate your biases toward each of these groups?

These questions are intended to compel you out of your comfort zone and help you embark on your journey toward self-awareness.

Step 2: Acquire Knowledge And Information

Self-awareness is only the first step toward achieving cultural competence. Knowledge acquisition, especially as it pertains to issues affecting underrepresented groups in your organization, is the second one. As a leader, you need to understand both the issues diverse employees face and the barriers limiting their access and success in the organization.

When working with diverse employees, you must realize that these individuals have complex identities. Therefore, you need to be aware of the effect that dimensions such as race, ethnicity, class, religion, age, sexual orientation, and physical ability, among others, can have on their worldview. Treat your employees as *many-layered multicultural selves* (personal communication, Janet Bennett, cofounder of the Intercultural Communications Institute, 2003), and all layers of their identities need to be considered, not just, for example, their ethnicity, sexual orientation, or nationality. An employee is not just female, just Muslim, or just African American. She is an *intersection* (Crenshaw 1989) of all these and many other identities.

As a leader, you also need to recognize that cultural differences can affect behavior. Culturally competent leaders know and understand US cultural values and how they differ from those of other countries. As discussed in Chapter 5, values such as independence and self-reliance are typical of individualistic cultures, such as the United States, and not necessarily part of other cultures' value systems. A hiring manager who is a direct communicator (see Chapter 3) may take lightly the potential of candidates whose "indirect" communication style compels them to understate their achievements. It would pay handsomely for global organizations to create learning opportunities so employees can understand important cultural differences and acquire the skills necessary for their interactions to result in the best possible outcomes.

Step 3: Acquire The Relational Skills For Working Effectively Across Differences

To work well with diverse employees and customers, leaders need significant relationship-building skills. Your employees need to know they matter to the organization, and you can demonstrate that by showing concern, being welcoming and putting them at ease, listening attentively, asking clarifying questions, showing patience, monitoring verbal and nonverbal behavior, gathering detailed information for following up, and showing empathy (Dreasher 2010).

Please note that one or two training programs designed to increase your knowledge of effective relational skills are not enough to develop cultural competence. You will need to increase your comfort level in working with differences, and this will take daily and persistent practice. The more comfortable you are with differences, the more effective you will be when working with diverse populations. The framework discussed below will help you understand how you view and deal with cultural differences.

A Framework For Diversity Development

A commonly referenced framework designed to help individuals become aware of, understand, and develop the skills to value differences is Milton Bennett's Developmental Model of Intercultural Sensitivity or DMIS (Bennett 1986, 1993, 1998).

The DMIS, organized along a continuum of six developmental stages (see Figure 9.1), is used to assess how individuals respond to cultural differences in nationality, ethnicity, gender, age, sexual orientation, religion, and any other differences learned or shared by a group of individuals (Bennett 2003).

FIGURE 9.1: The Developmental Model Of Intercultural Sensitivity

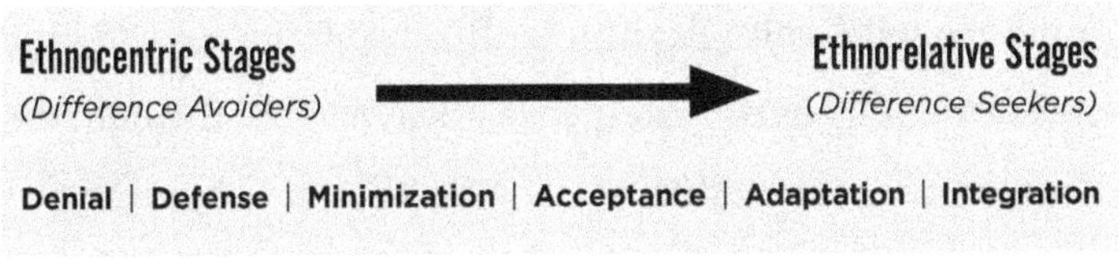

This is a visual representation of the model presented in Bennett (1998) and Bennett (2003).

Behavior and attitude toward differences determines where a person falls on the continuum. Individuals in the first three stages tend to be difference avoiders and have an ethnocentric perspective. In other words, they use their own cultural lens to view other orientations. Those in the last three stages are difference seekers; their ethnorelative perspective allows them to see their own culture in the context of other cultures (Bennett 2003). Training coordinators could use this model to a) help employees understand where they are on the continuum regarding their level of intercultural sensitivity and b) develop stage-appropriate interventions that facilitate development into the next stage.

A Brief Explanation Of The Different Stages

Denial of cultural differences. In this stage, individuals are unaware that certain types of differences exist. They either don't recognize cultural differences or, at best, only see broad, stereotypical categories. For example, when they think about Africa, the only images that come to mind are wild animals, jungle, Black people, or poverty. Chimamanda Ngozi Adichie warns us against the dangers of having a single story (i.e., thinking of Nigerians as only living in huts) in her 2009 TED Talk. She argued that "single stories create stereotypes and stereotypes are incomplete because they become the *only* story." Constantly thinking of other cultures in stereotypical ways reduces them to a simplistic model and robs them of all the other possibilities that could be.

Defense against cultural differences. Those defensive about cultural issues do recognize differences; however, they label the norms, values, and behaviors that differ from their own negatively. They demonstrate an us-versus-them mentality in which they see their culture as superior to others. Cultural differences tend to be challenging for individuals at this stage. Denigration and overt negative stereotyping are also likely in the defense stage. The most common strategy to counter the threat of difference is to negatively evaluate it—often with undesirable characteristics being attributed to every member of a distinct group.

Minimization of cultural differences. Individuals who minimize differences hold the general belief that, deep down, we are all the same. As a result, they may think that they do not have to do the difficult work of recognizing [their] own cultural patterns, understanding others, and eventually making the necessary adaptations (J. M. Bennett 2009). They expect culturally diverse employees to adapt their ways to those of the dominant culture. Color blindness is a typical mind frame of individuals in the minimization stage. It is imperative that leaders and employees examine their own culture so they can start contrasting it with other cultures.

Acceptance of differences. This is the gateway to inclusiveness, so to speak. Acceptance of differences shifts individuals from difference avoiders to difference seekers. Individuals at this stage recognize differences in values, norms, and beliefs and are interested in learning more about the diverse populations they serve so they can work more effectively with them. Cultural differences are relatively less threatening to these individuals, and they are able to suspend their judgment (at least temporarily), so they can understand the perspectives of others.

Adaptation to cultural differences. When ready to adapt to differences, individuals can change their behavior to interact effectively across differences. They know enough about their own culture as well as the culture of others to successfully code-shift (J. M. Bennett 2009) into the value scheme of others. They have the ability to operate in more than one cultural frame of reference and have highly developed inclusiveness and collaboration skills.

Integration of cultural differences. Reaching this stage can only be accomplished when individuals intentionally make a significant and sustained effort to become fully competent across differences. Those in this stage are truly bicultural or multicultural; they not only thrive on cultural differences, but they are also good at bridging differences. They can look at situations from multiple frames of reference and shift easily from one cultural frame to the other. These are the qualities of truly inclusive global leaders.

In any organization, expect that individuals will be at different stages on the DMIS continuum. Moving from one stage to the other will require a gradual, lifelong process of learning to be aware of and understanding cultural differences, as well as acquiring the necessary skills to work effectively across those differences. At the minimum, create opportunities so employees can operate at the *acceptance* stage because that is when they start understanding and valuing diversity.

It is important to understand that diversity development is an uncomfortable developmental process for most people because otherness, by its very nature, makes individuals uncomfortable (Chavez, Guido-DiBrito, and Mallory 2003). However, individuals need to push themselves out of their comfort zones and consistently seek opportunities to practice their relational skills. The more opportunities they have to deal with differences, the more comfortable they will be. The more comfortable they are, the better they will be at working across differences. In this case, the old saying is still true: practice will, indeed, make it perfect.

Once leaders embark on their journey from self-awareness to other awareness and to finally having the skills to adjust to the cultural orientation of others, they are more likely to behave like inclusive leaders. Gundling and Williams (2019) argue that inclusive leaders exhibit three essential characteristics:

a. **Empathy**: Being able to sense the emotions of others, including reactions to exclusion.

b. **Perspective:** Taking a broad and objective view of self and others.

c. **Flexibility**: Being able to switch their behavioral patterns so it takes other behaviors into consideration.

TIPS FOR WORKING EFFECTIVELY ACROSS DIFFERENCES

- Recognize and learn about cultural differences. This will not only strengthen your effectiveness, but will communicate respect for diverse employees. The opposite is also true; without a clear understanding of cultural differences, you run the risk of imposing your cultural orientation onto others.

- The more you learn about other cultures and value orientations, the more comfortable you will be around diversity. This, in turn, will increase your readiness to invite more diversity into the organization.

- Culturally competent leaders are: a) self-aware, b) knowledgeable of others, and c) have the skills to adjust their behavior to the cultural orientation of others.

- The path to cultural competence starts within. By starting this process internally, you are able to recognize that your own perspective is not the only (or necessarily the most valid) one, which allows for the acceptance of different perspectives.

- As a leader, you need to create learning opportunities so employees can understand important cultural differences and acquire the skills necessary so their interactions will result in the best possible outcomes.

- Constantly thinking of other cultures in stereotypical ways reduces them to a simplistic model and robs them of all the other possibilities that could be.

- Acceptance of differences shifts individuals from difference avoiders to difference seekers. Individuals at this stage recognize differences in values, norms, and beliefs and are interested in learning more about the diverse populations they serve so they can work more effectively with them.

- Truly inclusive global leaders can look at situations from multiple frames of reference and shift easily from one cultural frame to another.

- Understand that recognizing and valuing differences can be an uncomfortable developmental journey because differences can, sometimes, make individuals uncomfortable.

CHAPTER 10

Creating Truly Inclusive Global Organizations

For all practical purposes, all business today is global. Those individual businesses, firms, industries, and whole societies that clearly understand the new rules of doing business in a world economy will prosper; those that do not will perish.

—Ian Mitrof

Consider The Following Scenario

Masaru, a software engineer from Japan, was one of a few international engineers brought to IBM as part of a new exchange program. He was excited to have been selected for this elite program and was looking forward to rotating within the company's divisions for the duration of the program. In month four of his two-year stay in the United States, he finds himself questioning his decision to apply to the program.

Masaru is an introvert, and because he feels his English is still not good, he has developed a tendency to think carefully before making any contributions to his team's discussions. His own cultural background reinforces this behavior. Out of respect for his colleagues and superiors, he spends extra time formulating his answers before verbalizing them. He has started to notice, though, that the long pauses in his conversations tend to unnerve his colleagues.

Despite the fact that Masaru's qualifications make him a great addition to this particular project, he finds it difficult to contribute during team meetings. He is particularly intimidated by the communication style of his colleagues who seem to enjoy debating every nuance of the project and expressing their thoughts passionately. Although he is able to follow the technical aspects of the conversations, he has yet to make insightful contributions to the weekly meetings.

What should a team leader, who aims to be inclusive, do in this situation?

The problem in this scenario comes from two fronts: 1) the team includes both native- and non-native English speakers at different levels of proficiency, and 2) their communication styles are different. Masaru's personality is also a contributing factor. Clearly, this team is in need of a more effective strategy so all individuals can fully contribute.

A leader aiming to create a more inclusive team environment needs to ensure that every member can join in the discussion by monitoring the conversations, gauging everyone's level of involvement, and paying close attention to those who could still contribute but have yet to do so.

The animated exchanges among those who are fluent in English serve to discourage Masaru (and others like him) from fully contributing to the project. Until Masaru is confident enough in his ability to participate, his team leader will have to employ strategies that allow all members to participate, albeit their differences in style and personality. This may require her to step in to ask the more active participants to make room for others. She may also have to consider the possibility of more low-risk strategies, such as allowing Masaru to voice his opinion via email (this will give him extra time to formulate his thoughts) or in a private conversation. If she chooses the latter, she needs to remember that silence is part of Masaru's communication style and not necessarily a breakdown in the conversation.

The Need For Inclusion

There is no denying that globalization has changed the way we do business. In fact, organizations big and small are having to rethink their strategy and their parochial mindset (Cohen 2007, 177). Nowadays, global business ventures must be considered from a multi-contextual lens, not only from the perspective of the home culture but from that of the host culture as well. For example, will the company name or slogan mean the same when translated into the local language? Will the products be received the same way? When IKEA, the leading Swedish furniture retailer, first entered the United States, it replicated the formula that propelled its success in Sweden. However, it wasn't until the company changed its offerings to meet the specific needs of its US consumers that sales pivoted for the better (Gupta & Govindarajan 2001).

In Chapter 1, I discussed the need for creating inclusive organizations. Organizations where inclusion is embedded in their fabric reap many benefits, as Gundling and Williams (2019) attested. They found that inclusive organizations become more innovative, are able to grow their markets, have a better business outcome, are twice as likely to exceed their financial targets, and are able to retain top talent worldwide. Inclusive organizations require leaders with an inclusive mindset. However, becoming an inclusive leader requires individuals to challenge themselves so they can fully accept others with all their strengths and weaknesses (Bortini, Paci, Risi, and Rojnik 2016). This is no easy task, and it needs to be undertaken as a continuing developmental journey.

Inclusive leaders champion inclusion in all aspects of the organization—from recruitment, retention, and employee performance and evaluation to resource distribution, company culture, and more. These individuals go out of their way to:

- support, mentor, and sponsor diverse employees
- adapt their leadership style to meet the needs of diverse employees and clients
- create a safe space where employees feel empowered to speak up without fear of being penalized
- promote diverse talent by making sure they are involved in visible projects
- prevent *silos* and facilitate team interaction
- ensure everyone in the organization understands the impact of unconscious bias

Inclusive leaders are quick to address inappropriate behaviors (i.e., offensive jokes, hurtful comments) but do it in a way that invites dialogue. They also run their organization with laser-sharp focus; they are acutely aware of what is happening and intervene when needed. For example, they notice who is interrupting whom in the staff meeting, who is participating and who is not, and take measures to mitigate those situations. Above all, they recognize and embrace the business case for inclusion.

The Inclusive *Global* Leader (IGL)

In a global organization, inclusive leaders need to approach their responsibility with their global lenses. This requires shifting their frame from inclusive leadership to inclusive *global* leadership.

In addition to what was discussed above, IGLs recognize and embrace differences. In fact, teams cannot begin to enhance communication without first recognizing and then understanding and respecting cross-cultural differences (Brislin 1981). Many misunderstandings in a global environment are due to ignorance of cultural differences rather than a rejection of those differences (Adler and Gundersen 2008, 145).

IGLs never project their culture onto others. For example, a manager who prefers a hands-off approach may discover that a hands-on approach may be more appropriate with certain employees. This recognition is essential in identifying those with leadership potential in the organization. In fact, it is argued that our tendency is to look for ourselves when identifying future leadership prospects. This approach is fundamentally flawed in organizations with a diverse global workforce (Gundling and Williams 2019, 123).

IGLs value diversity of perspectives and proactively seek input from those who do not think like them. This is especially important when expanding into new markets and determining the psyche of new customers. In this case, tapping the insights of employees whose backgrounds are similar to the customer is vital. They recognize that the best solutions come by integrating multiple perspectives.

IGLs prevent misunderstandings because they are experts in style-switching, which allows them to deal more effectively with culturally conditioned behaviors. For example, they can recognize a disagreement in the polite responses of more indirect communicators who are not comfortable in committing to a project, but their cultural orientation prevents them from saying so directly. They also take on the role of *culture guides* since they are able to explain why things are done a particular way in a different cultural setting, which, in turn, assists others with frame-shifting (Gundling, Hogan, and Cvitkovich 2011). Overall, IGLs:

- are self- and other-aware
- are good at bridging cultural differences
- see situations from multiple perspectives
- recognize and value different beliefs and behaviors
- are curious to learn about cultural differences, and
- adapt their behavior to work with different value orientations

Above all, IGLs recognize the necessity to think globally but act locally when the need arises.

Creating An Inclusive Global Organization

What kinds of organizational changes need to happen to create a truly inclusive global organization?

First and foremost, executive engagement is essential. If the leadership is not committed, inclusion initiatives will inevitably fail. In fact, in the absence of sustained executive commitment, other priorities ultimately take precedence, and the focus on inclusion fades, leaving a deep layer of skepticism throughout the employee population (Gundling and Williams 2019, 190). In addition to showing support, leadership also needs to communicate the benefits of a diverse and inclusive organization, set expectations, and create a sense of urgency. It is important to understand that, although inclusion initiatives start at the top, everyone in the organization needs to play an active role in creating an inclusive environment.

IGOs hire for culture add, not culture fit. Organizations today are not only competing for top talent, but they also want to safeguard that those who are brought in will add to the organization. Competing successfully for top talent, though, means more than simply hiring the most capable individuals. IGOs need their new recruits to support the organization's growth and serve diverse clients wherever the company operates.

As far as diversity is concerned, spending time and energy looking for the *best fit* instead of *culture fit* rarely yields positive results. In fact, many have argued that culture fit is the equivalent of a candidate having passed the beer test. In other words, this is someone you would want to hang out with (Dreasher 2019, 2018; Reilly 2016). The problem with this strategy is that, while your newly found beer buddy may indeed be able to do the job, hiring for culture fit inevitably gets in the way of increasing diversity in the organization. If this is your goal, though, you need to ban culture fit as a reason for rejecting a candidate—because it is often code for *you don't look, act, or think like us*. More worrisome is that this attitude also indicates unconscious bias is at play. While there are laws in place that prevent companies from openly discriminating against candidates on the basis of race, gender, or religious affiliation, for example, we all know it is still happening. If your goal is to increase workplace diversity, look instead for cultural add in candidates. This allows the organization to bring in candidates who can truly help ***shape*** the culture of the organization, rather than fit into it.

You also need a culturally competent recruiting team. In Chapter 9, I discussed cultural competence as the need for a) self-awareness, b) knowledge of others, and c) the ability to adjust behavior to the cultural orientation of others (Dreasher 2010). Knowledge of culture-based behavior patterns can be important not only for dealing with international candidates but also for making accurate judgments about diverse styles of work and communication within the same country (Gundling and Williams 2019, 189). An interviewer may fully expect a candidate to showcase their experiences and skills to sell himself, only to be faced with the reality that the expected bragging never takes place. The candidate, on the other hand, is counting on the fact that his strong track record of achievements will speak for themselves. Recruiting teams need to recognize instances when their own cultural orientation may lead them to misinterpret the behavior of qualified candidates who could, if given the opportunity, lead the organization to great success in the global market.

IGOs are adamant about setting business priorities, devising plans for growth, and using data to measure progress. How else will they know when they have arrived at their set destination? While it is easy to measure the number of women, minorities, or people of various nationalities in leadership positions, Gundling and Williams (2019, 197) warn us about the dangers of categorizing people in a global organization:

> *[N]o one is just female, or just Black, or just Muslim. Each person is a whole package of interlocking attributes. Employees with multicultural backgrounds may also be reluctant to identify with any single nationality—this would force them to choose between parents or between their current homes and their countries of origin. LGBTQ employees in some countries may push for non-binary gender*

categories, while in other places these categories are illegal. Racial classifications such as "white," "Black," or "Asian" may fail to take into account differences in educational opportunities or socioeconomic backgrounds.

Although it is convenient to have clear and straightforward ways to categorize employees for statistical purposes, the *intersectionality* (Crenshaw 1989) of their identities—not to mention that data collected says nothing about the more invisible traits such as personality, cognitive style, personal values, etc.—makes this process far more complex. Perhaps, more meaningful ways of tracking progress toward inclusion could include questions such as:

- Who is advancing in the organization? Who is not? Is there a difference in gender, ethnicity, nationality, function, etc.?

- Does the demographic profile of employees reflect the profile of the organization's customers or suppliers?

- How are individuals experiencing the organization? Is there a difference based on gender, race, ethnicity, nationality, rank, etc.?

- Which groups are leaving the organization at a higher rate?

- Are groups promoted the same way? Who is falling behind, and at what point in their careers?
- Is the organization committed to equal pay for those in the same job category?
- How diverse is the leadership?

Concluding Thoughts

Knowledge of culture-specific behavior, as the numerous examples I shared throughout this book, is useful, but you have to keep in mind that it will never apply to all individuals or circumstances. This, in fact, leads to stereotyping. Thiederman (1991) argues that proper behaviors are those that are appropriate in the context of the culture, setting, and occasion; what is right in one set of circumstances may not be appropriate in another.

In order to lead inclusively, you need highly developed observational skills. How far apart do individuals stand? How do they greet each other? Who participates freely in staff meetings, and who doesn't? Do these behaviors change depending on the context (i.e., business setting only)? It is equally important to understand that we always look at situations from our own ethnocentric perspective. That is, we look at situations through our own culturally-tinted glasses, and we need to compensate for the cultural distortions they cause (Thiederman 1991). Remember our tendency to evaluate our norms and values as appropriate and to make negative judgments about someone else's norms and values. When you find yourself attaching a negative interpretation to someone else's behavior, first consider if culture has anything to do with it.

While you may expect similarities (i.e., all humans have common needs for food, shelter, and security), your employees' unique cultural upbringing will determine what is appropriate for them and how they behave. Culturally competent leaders understand that and work diligently to build bridges across those differences.

Lastly, if you do not notice, learn about, and acquire the skills to master cultural differences, misunderstandings will most certainly occur. This, in turn, will greatly compromise the effectiveness of a global, inclusive organization.

References

Adichie, Chimamanda N. 2009. "The Danger of a Single Story." *TED Global.* https://www.ted.com/talks/chimamanda_ngozi_adichie_the_danger_of_a_single_story.

Adler, Nancy, and Allison Gundersen. 2008. *International Dimensions Of Organizational Behavior.* Mason, OH: South-Western.

"Advancing African American Women in the Workplace: What Managers Need to Know." *Catalyst,* February 15, 2004. https://www.catalyst.org/research/advancing-african-american-women-in-the-workplace-what-managers-need-to-know/.

Axtell, Roger E. 1991. *Gestures: Do's and Taboos of Body Language Around the World.* New York: John Wiley & Sons, Inc.

Belyh, Anastasia. 2019. "Understanding Cultures and People With Hofstede Dimensions." *Cleverism*, September 20, 2019. https://www.cleverism.com/understanding-cultures-people-hofstede-dimensions/.

Bertrand, Marianne, and Sendhil Mullainathan. 2004. "Are Emily and Greg More Employable than Lakisha and Jamal? A Field Experiment on Labor Market Discrimination." *American Economic Review* 94(4):991–1013.

Bhasin, Hitesh. 2020. "5 Advantages of Market Competition to End Customers." *Marketing91,* January 25, 2020. https://www.marketing91.com/5-advantages-of-market-competition/.

Billings-Harris, Lenora. 1998. *The Diversity Advantage: A Guide to Making Diversity Work.* Winchester, OH: Oak Hill Press.

Birdwhistell, Ray L. 1955. "Background to Kinesics." *ETC: A Review of General Semantics,* 13(1):10–18.

Bortini, Paola, Angelica Paci, Anne Rise, and Irene Rojnik. 2016. *Inclusive Leadership: Theoretical Framework.* School for Leaders Foundation, EU Fundraising Association. file:///d:/book%20-%20mastering%20cultural%20differences/chapter%2010%20-%20the%20global%20leader/inclusive_leadership.pdf.

Brislin, Richard. 1981. *Cross-Cultural Encounters.* New York: Pergamon.

Brislin, Richard. 1994. "Individualism and Collectivism as the Source of Many Specific Cultural Differences." In *Improving Intercultural Interactions: Modules for Cross-Cultural Training Programs,* edited by Richard Brislin and Tomoko Yoshida, 71–88. Thousand Oaks, CA: Sage Publications.

Bucher, Richard D, and Patricia L. Bucher. 2008. *Building Cultural Intelligence: Nine Megaskills.* Upper Saddle River, NJ: Pearson Prentice Hall.

Bennett, Milton J. 1986. "A Developmental Approach To Training For Intercultural Sensitivity." *International Journal of Intercultural Relations* 10(2):179–196.

Bennet, Milton J. 1993. "Towards Ethnorelativism: A Developmental Model of Intercultural Sensitivity." In *Education for the Intercultural Experience,* edited by Michael Paige, 21–71. Yarmouth, ME: Intercultural Press.

Bennet, Milton J. 1998. "Intercultural Communication: A Current Perspective." In *Basic Concepts Of Intercultural Communication: Selected Readings,* edited by Milton J. Bennet, 1–34, Yarmouth, ME: Intercultural Press.

Bennett, Janet M. 2003. "Turning Frogs Into Interculturalists: A Student-Centered Developmental Approach to Teaching Intercultural Competence." In *Crossing Cultures: Insights from Master Teachers,* edited by Nakiye Boyacigiller, Richard Goodman, and Margaret Phillips, 157–170. New York: Routledge.

Bennett, Janet M. 2009. "Transformative Training: Designing Programs for Culture Learning." In *Contemporary Leadership and Intercultural Competence: Exploring Cross-Cultural Dynamics Within Organizations,* edited by Michael A. Moodian, 95–110. Thousand Oaks, CA: Sage.

Carpenter, Mason S. 2002. "The Implications of Strategy and Social Context for the Relationship Between Top Management Team Heterogeneity and Firm Performance." *Strategic Management Journal* 23(3):275–284.

Carr-Ruffino, Norma. 2015. *Managing Diversity.* New York: Pearson Learning Solutions.

Chavez, Alicia F., Florence Guido-DiBrito, and Sherry L. Mallory. 2003. "Learning to Value the 'Other': A Framework of Individual Diversity Development." *Journal of College Student Development* 44(4):453–469.

Cohen, Ed. 2007. *Leadership Without Borders: Successful Strategies from World-Class Leaders.* Hoboken, NJ: John Wiley & Sons.

"The Cost of Employee Turnover Due Solely to Unfairness in the Workplace." 2007. *Level Playing Field Institute.* https://www.smash.org/wp-content/uploads/2015/05/corporate-leavers-survey.pdf.

Cox, Taylor H., Sharon A. Lobel, and Poppy L. McLeod. 1991. "Effects of Ethnic Group, Cultural Differences, Uncooperative and Competitive Behavior on a Group Task." *Academy of Management Journal* 34(4):827–847.

Cox Jr., Taylor, and Carol Smolinski. 1994. *Managing Diversity and Glass Ceiling Initiatives as National Economic Imperatives.* Ann Arbor: The University of Michigan.

Crenshaw, Kimberle. 1989. "Demarginalizing the Intersection of Race and Sex: A Black Feminist Critique of Antidiscrimination Doctrine, Feminist Theory and Antiracist Politics." *University of Chicago Legal Forum*, 1(8). https://chicagounbound. uchicago.edu/cgi/viewcontent.cgi?article=1052&context=uclf.

Crockett, Joan. 1999. "Diversity: Winning Competitive Advantage Through a Diverse Workforce." *HR Focus* 76(5):9–11.

DeVito, Joseph A. 1989. *The Nonverbal Communication Workbook.* Prospect Heights, IL: Waveland Press.

Dreasher, Luiza M. 2018. *Cultural Competence in Academic Advising: Skills for Working Effectively Across Differences,* 2nd edition, Pocket Guide Series (PG16). Manhattan: National Academic Advising Association.

Dreasher, Luiza M. 2018. "Communication is About More than Words." *The Inclusion Solution,* June 21, 2018. http://www. theinclusionsolution.me/point-view-communication-words/.

Dreasher, Luiza M. 2018. "Want to Bring Diversity In? Stop Looking for the Best Fit." *The Inclusion Solution,* December 6, 2018. http://www.theinclusionsolution.me/point-view-want-bring-diversity-stop-looking-best-fit/.

Dreasher, Luiza M. 2017. "Are Your Biases and Lack of Cultural Understanding Keeping Diversity Out?" *The Inclusion Solution,* May 4, 2017. http://www.theinclusionsolution.me/point-view-biases-lack-cultural-understanding-keeping-diversity-out/.

Dreasher, Luiza M. 2019. "Let's Get Practical: Successful Strategies for Recruiting and Retaining a Diverse Workforce." *The Inclusion Solution,* June 27, 2019. http://www.theinclusionsolution.me/lets-get-practical-successful-strategies-for-recruiting-and-retaining-a-diverse-workforce/.

Dreasher, Luiza M. 2017. "Acknowledging Differences is the First Step Toward Effective Diversity Management." *The Inclusion Solution,* July 7, 2017. http://www.theinclusionsolution.me/point-view-acknowledging-differences-first-step-toward-effective-diversity-management/.

Dreasher, Luiza M. 2010. "Preparing advisors to work effectively across differences: A three-step framework." In *Comprehensive Advisor Training and Development: Practices That Deliver,* 2nd edition, edited by Givans Voller, Marsha Miller, and Susan Neste, 155–169. Manhattan: National Academic Advising Association.

EEOC Press Release. 2019. "Halliburton to Pay $275,000 to Settle National Origin and Religious Discrimination Suit," October 8, 2019. https://www.eeoc.gov/newsroom/halliburton-pay-275000-settle-national-origin-and-religious-discrimination-suit.

Eisenberger, Robert, Peter Fasolo, and Valerie Davis-LaMastro. 1990. "Perceived Organizational Support and Employee Diligence, Commitment, and Innovation." *Journal of Applied Psychology* 75(1):51–59.

Ely, Robin J., and David A. Thomas. 2001. "Cultural Diversity at Work: The Moderating Effects of Work Group Perspectives on Diversity." *Administrative Science Quarterly* 46:229–273.

Farfan, Barbara. 2019. "Apple's Retail Stores Around the World." *The Balance*, May 30, 2019. https://www.thebalancesmb.com/apple-retail-stores-global-locations-2892925.

Gill, Cassandra. 2017. "Hofstede's Cultural Dimensions and Differences Across Cultures." *OUPblog,* March 23, 2017. https://blog.oup.com/2017/03/hofstede-cultural-dimensions/.

Gudykunst, William B. 2004. *Bridging Differences: Effective Intergroup Communication.* Thousand Oaks, CA: Sage.

Gudykunst, William B., and Yuko Matsumoto. 1996. "Cross-Cultural Variability of Communication in Personal Relationships." In *Communication in personal relationships across cultures,* edited by William Gudykunst, Stella Ting-Toomey, and Tsukasa Nishida, 19–56. Thousand Oaks, CA: Sage.

Gundling, Ernest, and Cheryl Williams. 2019. *Inclusive Leadership: From Awareness to Action.* Aperian Global, Kindle Edition.

Gundling, Ernest, Terry Hogan, and Karen Cvitkovich. 2011. *What is Global Leadership? 10 Key Behaviors that Define Successful Global Leaders.* Boston: Nicholas Brealey Publishing.

Gupta, Anil K., Vijay Govindarajan, and Haiyan Wang. 2001. *The Quest for Global Dominance: Transforming Global Presence Into Global Competitive Advantage.* San Francisco: Jossey Bass.

Hall, Edward T. 1983. *The Dance of Life: The Other Dimension of Time.* New York: Anchor Books.

Hall, Edward T. 1976. *Beyond Culture.* New York: Anchor Books.

Hoeller, Sophie-Claire. 2015. "25 common American customs that are considered offensive in other countries." *Business Insider,* August 5, 2015. www.businessinsider.com/american-customs-that-are-offensive-abroad-2015-8.

Hofstede, Geert. 1980. *Culture's Consequences: International Differences in Work-Related Values.* Beverly Hills: Sage Publications.

Hofstede, Geert. 1984. "The Cultural Relativity of the Quality of Life Concept." *Academy of Management Review* 9(3):389–398.

Hofstede, Geet. 1991. *Cultures and Organizations: Software of the Mind.* London: McGraw-Hill.

Hofstede, Geert. 2001. *Culture's Consequences: Comparing Values, Behaviors, Institutions, and Organizations Across Nations,* 2nd edition. Thousand Oaks, CA: Sage Publications.

Hofstede, Geert, Gert Jan Hofstede, and Michael Minkov. 2010. *Cultures and Organizations: Software of the Mind,* 3rd edition. New York: McGraw-Hill.

Hsu, Francis L. K. 1981. *Americans and Chinese: Passage to Differences,* 3rd edition. Honolulu: University of Hawaii Press.

Humphreys, Jeffrey M. 2019. *The Multicultural Economy.* University of Georgia: Terry College of Business.

"Implicit Association Test." *Project Implicit.* https://implicit.harvard.edu/implicit/

"7 Trends for Workforce 2020: How to Make Today's Ever-Changing Workplace Work for You." *Instructure,* 2016. https://sewi-atd.org/resources/Pictures/7%20TRENDS%20FOR%20WORKFORCE%202020.pdf

Knorr, Andreas, and Andreas Arndt. 2003. "Why Did Wal-Mart Fail in Germany?" Institute for World Economics and International Management 24:1–35.

Lambert, Jonamay, and Selma Meyers. 1994. *50 Activities for Diversity Training.* Amherst, MA: Human Resource Development Press.

Losey, Michael R. 1993. "Is Sexual Orientation an Issue in the Workplace?" *HR News* 12:16–17.

Maharaj, Davan. 2000. "Coca-Cola to Settle Racial Bias Lawsuit." *Los Angeles Times,* November 17, 2000. https://www.latimes.com/archives/la-xpm-2000-nov-17-mn-53405-story.html.

Martin, Judith N., and Thomas K. Nakayama. 2000. *Intercultural Communication in Contexts.* New York: McGraw-Hill.

Marx, Elizabeth. 2001. *Breaking Through Culture Shock: What You Need to Succeed in International Business.* Yarmouth, ME: Intercultural Press.

Mayo, Margarita. 1999. "Capitalizing on a Diverse Workforce." *Ivey Business Journal* 64(1):20–27.

Mehrabian, Albert, and Susan R. Ferris. 1967. "Inference of Attitudes from Nonverbal Communication in Two Channels." *Journal of Consulting Psychology* 31(3):248–252.

Miller, Hannah. 2020. "Prada Reaches Settlement with NYC Over 'Racist Iconography' in Window Display." CNBC, February 5, 2020. https://www.cnbc.com/2020/02/05/prada-settlement-with-nyc-over-racist-iconography-in-window-display.html.

"Minority Markets Have $3.9 Trillion Buying Power." 2019. *The Multicultural Economy Report*, March 21, 2019. https://www.newswise.com/articles/minority-markets-have-3-9-trillion-buying-power.

Morrison, Terri, and Wayne Conaway. 2011. *Kiss, Bow, or Shake Hands: Sales and Marketing.* New York: McGraw-Hill.

Morrison, Terri, and Wayne Conaway. 2006. *Kiss, Bow, or Shake Hands.* Avon, MA: Adams Media.

Moss-Racusin, Corrinne A., John F. Dovidio, Victoria L. Brescoll, Mark Graham, and Jo Handelsman. 2012. "Science Faculty's Subtle Gender Biases Favor Male Students." *PNAS,* October 9, 2012. 109(41):16474–16479. doi.org/10.1073/pnas. 1211286109.

Nemeth, Charlan J. 1986. "Differential Contributions of Majority and Minority Influence." *Psychological Review* 93(1):23–32.

Nemeth, Charlan J., and Joel Wachtler. 1983. "Creative Problem Solving as a Result of Majority vs. Minority Influence." *European Journal of Social Psychology* 13:45–55.

"Proven Strategies for Addressing Unconscious Bias in the Workplace." 2008. *Diversity Best Practices* 2(5):1–20.

Richard, Orlando C. 2017. "Racial Diversity, Business Strategy, and Firm Performance: A Resource-Based View." *Academy of Management Journal*, November 30, 2017. 43(2):164–178. doi.org/10.5465/1556374.

Ricks, David A. 2006. *Blunders in International Business*. Malden: Blackwell Publishing.

Reilly, Kate. 2016. "Ban the Term 'Culture Fit' and Other Great Diversity Tips From Pandora." *LinkedIn Talent Blog*, December 14, 2016. https://business.linkedin.com/talent-solutions/blog/diversity/2016/ban-the-term-culture-fit-and-other-great-diversity-tips-from-pandora.

Salomon, Mary F., and Joan A. Schork. 2003. "Turn Diversity to Your Advantage." *Research Technology Management* 46(4):37–44. doi:10.1080/08956308.2003.11671575.

Samovar, Larry A., and Richard E. Porter. 1997. *Intercultural Communication: A Reader*. Belmont, CA: Wadsworth Publishing Company.

Singelis, Ted. 1994. "Nonverbal Communication in Intercultural Interactions." In *Improving Intercultural Interactions: Modules for Cross-Cultural Training Programs*, edited by Richard Brislin and Tomoko Yoshida, 268–294. Thousand Oaks, CA: Sage Publications.

Schell, Michael, and Sean Dubberke. 2018. "The Change Tolerance Dimension: How to Lead Multicultural Workplace Teams Through Changing Times." *CultureWizard*, September 17, 2018. https://www.rw-3.com/blog/the-change-tolerance-dimension-how-to-lead-multi-cultural.

"Symbolism of Colors and Color Meanings Around the World." *Shutterstock*, April 3, 2015. https://www.shutterstock.com/blog/color-symbolism-and-meanings-around-the-world.

Solomon, Charlene M., and Michael S. Schell. 2009. *Managing Across Cultures: The Seven Keys to Doing Business with a Global Mindset.* Thousand Oaks, CA: Sage Publications.

Spitzberg, Brian H., and Gabrielle Changnon. 2009. "Conceptualizing Intercultural Competence." In *The SAGE Handbook of Intercultural Competence,* edited by Darla K. Deardorff, 2–52. Thousand Oaks, CA: Sage Publications.

Storti, Craig. 1999. *Figuring Foreigners Out: A Practical Guide.* Yarmouth, ME: Intercultural Press.

Thiederman, Sondra. 2003. *Making Diversity Work: Seven Steps for Defeating Bias in The Workplace.* Chicago: Dearborn Trade Publishing.

Thiederman, Sondra. 1991. *Profiting in America's Multicultural Marketplace: How to Do Business Across Cultural Lines.* New York: Macmillan.

Ting-Toomey, Stella, and Leeva C. Chung. 2012. *Understanding Intercultural Communication.* New York: Oxford University Press.

Triandis, Harry C., Richard Brislin, and C. Harry Hui. 1988. "Cross-Cultural Training Across the Individualism-Collectivism Divide." *International Journal of Intercultural Relations* 12(3):269–289.

Vespa, Jonathan, David M. Armstrong, and Lauren Medina. 2020. "Demographic Turning Points for the United States: Population Projections for 2020 to 2060." U.S. Census Bureau. https://www.census.gov/content/dam/Census/library/publications/2020/demo/p25-1144.pdf.

Zimmerman, Ann, and Emily Nelson. 2006. "With Profit Elusive, Wal-Mart to Exit Germany." *The Wall Street Journal,* July 29, 2006. https://www.wsj.com/articles/SB115407238850420246.

Wang, Mary M., Richard Brislin, Wei-zhong Wang, David Williams, and Julie Haiyan Chao, 2000. *Turning Bricks into Jade: Critical Incidents for Mutual Understanding among Chinese and Americans.* Yarmouth: Intercultural Press.

Watson, Warren E., Kamalesh Kumar, and Larry K. Michaelsen. "Cultural Diversity's Impact on Interaction Process and Performance." *Academy of Management Journal* 36, no.3: 590–602.

Wolny, Nick. 2019. "The LGBTQ+ Community Has $3.7 Trillion In Purchasing Power; Here's How We Want You to Sell to Us." *Entrepreneur*, June 10, 2019. Retrieved from https://www.entrepreneur.com/article/334983

Acknowledgments

One of the first places I worked in the United States was at the International Resource Center (IRC) at Iowa State University—first as a graduate assistant and later as a director. The IRC, in my mind, was a combination of a warehouse and a museum. It housed artifacts and information from over 250 countries, and you could find anything, from a replica of a Korean crown encrusted with jade (quite possibly worth several thousand dollars) to chewing sticks from Ghana, to a headrest made by the Pekot tribe of Kenya, to a penis sheath worn by males in the West Sepik region of Papua New Guinea. These were some of the same artifacts that, many years later, I carried with me to conduct intercultural communication workshops to many audiences across the country. If this were a different book, I would go into detail about having to explain to TSA agents inspecting my luggage what a penis sheath was and why I had one in my suitcase. The IRC, no doubt, sparked my curiosity and interest in learning and then teaching about different cultures; it also cemented my conviction that building bridges across differences is essential. It was true back then, and it is certainly truer now in this global economy. I am forever grateful to

Margatertjean Weltha and Ruth Osborn for hiring me. I am certain that fateful day marked the beginning of my journey toward understanding cultural differences, and later, helping others understand those differences.

My initial intention of coming to the United States was simply to practice English. I was, after all, teaching English in Brazil. I would like to thank my mother, who fought valiantly for me until my father acquiesced and recognized the benefits of such an incredible experience. I also would like to recognize my late father, who, despite his reservations of allowing his only daughter to move to another country, made sure I would be supported by giving me all the family savings. I arrived in the United States with $190 to my name.

My three brothers, Silvio, Renato, and Fernando, were also instrumental in my journey. They supported and encouraged me to pursue my dreams. Decades later, Renato helped me see the light and encouraged me to pivot direction at a time I needed it the most. I know they will be rejoicing with me and helping me celebrate the publication of this book. And I am certain that my brother Silvio, although he was taken far too soon from his family, will be cheering my victory proudly and loudly as well.

I would be remiss if I did not thank my friend Maureen and her husband, José Valente. Valente had received a scholarship from the Brazilian government to pursue his PhD in the United States. Since Maureen and I had attended college together, they invited me to come with them to the United States to help take care of their newborn twins, Ana Claudia and Lívia, and, of course, practice English. Maureen and José, in my mind, were the masterminds behind my journey.

Another big thank you to my mother- and father-in-law, Louise and Lloyd Dreasher. They welcomed me (a foreigner) into their family and did so with open arms and hearts. David, Ron, and Laura are three of the kindest, friendliest, and most generous individuals I have ever met—all thanks to the good foundation the two of you laid for them.

It would have been an enormous challenge to complete this book without Henry DeVries' guidance. In October 2019, I had the privilege of attending an NSA-MN chapter meeting where Mark LeBlanc and Henry DeVries were guest speakers. Mark talked about writing the right book, and Henry talked about persuading with a story. Never in my wildest imagination had I thought I would one day write a book. At some point during that meeting, I gathered enough courage to approach Henry about the possibility of writing a book, and the rest, as they say, is history. I want to thank Henry for keeping me on track and for gently reminding me, "Luiza, this is not the book we agreed upon, remember?" every time I veered off the path. Henry, your guidance and support were invaluable.

My last thanks have to go to my readers for investing in this book. I honor and respect your ongoing commitment to mastering cultural differences.

About The Author

Luiza Dreasher has over twenty years of experience in the areas of diversity, inclusion, and cultural competence development. Her expertise in global and domestic diversity has led to consulting jobs and invitations to develop and implement customized programs to numerous audiences, including the United States Department of Defense, Pioneer Hi-Bred International, Schreiber Foods of Brazil, MN Department of Public Safety, and numerous institutions of higher education.

She has presented extensively nationwide on topics such as contrasting US- American values with those of other cultures, challenges and opportunities of a culturally diverse workplace, building inclusive environments, communicating effectively across cultures, resolving conflicts successfully, understanding cultural differences, and the importance of recruiting and retaining a culturally diverse workforce. In her most recent podcast, "You Hear Something Offensive, Then What? Strategies for Increasing Your Effectiveness Around Diversity," she shared the impact of microaggressions in the workplace and specific strategies individuals can use to speak up in a productive way.

Luiza has taught courses focusing on social justice, cross-cultural race relations, and currently teaches diversity management. While serving as an assistant dean and director of multicultural and international inclusion at Mitchell Hamline School of Law in Saint Paul, she developed and taught a course on cultural competence for the legal profession.

As a contributing writer for *The Inclusion Solution*, a newsletter distributed by The Winters Group, Luiza focuses on transformative solutions for equity, diversity, and inclusion in the workplace. With several thousand readers, Luiza has written about issues impacting today's organizations such as recruiting and retaining a diverse workforce, microaggressions in the workplace, achieving inclusive religious observance, age discrimination, and how biases and lack of cultural competence prevent diversity. She also wrote a paper on addressing race and racism in the workplace. More recently, she wrote "How Many More Have to Die? What Each and Every One of Us Can Do," written after the death of George Floyd in Minneapolis.

Luiza currently serves as the president and CEO of Mastering Cultural Differences. In that capacity, she designs and implements customized programs for organizations that want team members to understand and work well across cultural differences.

As a speaker, her message zeroes in on the importance of creating environments where all feel included and can thrive. As a result of her work, individuals often share they feel more at ease working across differences and report new levels of understanding and cooperation with the people they work alongside with, lead, and serve.

On a personal note, Luiza, her husband, his parents, and their two small children spent a week in the Amazon rainforest and loved it!

You can learn more about Luiza's training and speaking topics by visiting her website or sending her an email.

Website: www.masteringculturaldifferences.com
Email: luiza@masteringculturaldifferences.com

www.ingramcontent.com/pod-product-compliance
Lightning Source LLC
Chambersburg PA
CBHW031936190326
41519CB00007B/553
* 9 7 8 1 9 5 2 2 3 3 4 5 6 *